Endeavor

8

New Readers Press®

ProLiteracy's publishing division

The following teachers participated in pilot testing of Endeavor:

Evelyn Surma, Adult Education Teacher
Anaheim Union High School District, Anaheim, CA

Maria Pagnotta, ABE-GED Professor
Seminole Community College, Sanford, FL

Rachel M. Slavkin, Adjunct Faculty
Seminole Community College, Sanford, FL

Lora Zangari, Professional Development Coordinator
Lancaster Lebanon IU13, Lancaster, PA

Endeavor® 8
ISBN 978-1-56420-858-3

Proceeds from the sale of New Readers Press materials support professional
development, training, and technical assistance programs of ProLiteracy
that benefit local literacy programs in the U.S. and around the globe.

Contributing Author: Vista Resources, Inc.
Developmental Editors: Ellen Northcutt, Donna Townsend
Creative Director: Andrea Woodbury
Production Specialist: Maryellen Casey
Art and Design Supervisor: James P. Wallace
Illustrator: Carlotta Tormey, represented by Wilkinson Studios, Inc.

Contents

Lesson 1: Staying Fit and Healthy (Health) 5

Reading Strategies: Use what you know, visualize

Reading Skill: Make inferences

Word Building: Past tense verbs

Graphic Organizers: Inference diagram, idea web

Writing: Write a letter to the editor

Lesson 2: On the Job (Work) 15

Reading Strategies: Use what you know, make predictions

Reading Skill: Make judgments

Word Building: Plurals

Graphic Organizers: Judgment charts

Writing: Write an opinion

Lesson 3: We Are Family (Family) 25

Reading Strategies: Use what you know, ask yourself questions

Reading Skill: Synthesize information

Word Building: Root words

Graphic Organizers: Synthesis charts

Writing: Write an explanation

Lesson 4: Making a Comeback (Community) 35

Reading Strategies: Use what you know, set a purpose

Reading Skill: Identify main idea and details

Word Building: Prefixes *re-, mis-, im-, un-*

Graphic Organizers: Main idea and details charts

Writing: Write a personal narrative

Lesson 5: Summer Vacations (School and Education) 45

Reading Strategies: Use what you know, ask yourself questions

Reading Skill: Distinguish fact and opinion

Word Building: Suffixes *-al, -ful, -ness, -ly*

Graphic Organizers: Fact and opinion charts

Writing: Write a description

Lesson 6: Help in an Emergency (Civics and Government) 55

Reading Strategies: Make predictions, visualize

Reading Skill: Identify cause and effect

Word Building: Compound words

Graphic Organizers: Cause and effect diagram, summary chart

Writing: Write a summary

Lesson 7: A Sports Icon (Sports and Recreation) 65

Reading Strategies: Use what you know, summarize

Reading Skill: Recognize time order

Word Building: Comparative adjectives -er, -ier

Graphic Organizers: Time lines

Writing: Write about a person's life

Lesson 8: Flying High (Housing and Transportation) 75

Reading Strategies: Use what you know, ask yourself questions

Reading Skill: Draw conclusions

Word Building: Root words

Graphic Organizers: Conclusions charts

Writing: Write a letter to the editor

Lesson 9: Where Did That Fish Come From? (Food) 85

Reading Strategies: Use what you know, visualize

Reading Skill: Compare and contrast

Word Building: Prefixes *semi-, multi-, bi-, inter-, pre-*

Graphic Organizers: Venn diagrams

Writing: Write a comparison

Lesson 10: Spending and Saving (Consumerism and Money) 95

Reading Strategies: Use what you know, preview

Reading Skill: Classify information

Word Building: Suffixes *-scope, -ship, -less*

Graphic Organizers: Classification charts

Writing: Write a description

Answer Key 105

Staying Fit and Healthy

Learning Objectives

In this lesson you will:

▧ Learn about weight lifting and steroid use.

▧ Make inferences about what you read.

▧ Master the key vocabulary used in the story.

▧ Write a letter to the editor about steroid use.

Key Vocabulary

contorting *(verb)* twisting out of the usual form

ecstatic *(adjective)* thrilled

faithfully *(adverb)* regularly

icons *(noun)* people who are recognized as worthy of great respect

inwardly *(adverb)* in the mind

obsession *(noun)* an extreme interest in something that keeps you from thinking about other things

smirk *(noun)* a smile that shows satisfaction with yourself

specimens *(noun)* examples of something from a group of similar things

surveyed *(verb)* looked over in a careful way

unaccountable *(adjective)* not easily explained

Before You Read

Active readers often take a quick look at a story and ask themselves, What do I already know about this subject? Readers who connect what they know to what they are about to read better understand what they read. Another good active reading strategy is visualizing. When you form pictures in your mind of what you are reading, you may be able to remember the story better.

Use what you know.

1. Do you know anyone who has used steroids? If so, what was the effect?

   _____

   _____

   _____

2. What have you heard about the use of steroids in sports?

   _____

   _____

   _____

   _____

3. Do you think the use of steroids ought to be illegal?

   _____

   _____

   _____

   _____

Visualize while you read.

1. How do you think Tim feels based on the first paragraph?

   _____

   _____

   _____

The Rage

Are steroids the answer to Tim's problem? Highlight or underline phrases that tell how Tim and Ox each look.

Tim felt his biceps and frowned. He'd been weight lifting for months now, **faithfully** showing up at the gym four times a week to lift the ever-increasing weights. His muscles, though, didn't look nearly as impressive as he'd hoped they would by now.

5 Discouraged, he sat on the weight bench and idly watched as the guy they called Ox accepted a small package from the gym owner and handed over a wad of cash.

Ox was one of the most remarkable physical **specimens** at the gym. His muscles looked chiseled from marble, and he swaggered around like he owned

10 the place. He knew he looked fine. "Yeah," thought Tim, "and unless I'm an idiot, he's buying those muscles by popping steroids."

Tim kept staring at Ox. He watched the man strut. Tim wanted a body like that. Abruptly, he got up and walked over to him. "Ox," Tim said.

"Yo?" said Ox, rubbing his forearm as he stared at it. It was impressive,

15 Tim thought, staring too. He paused for a second, not sure how to approach this subject.

"I saw you get some stuff from Paul," Tim said. "You juicing up? If you are, I want in. You are looking fine, my friend."

Ox turned his attention from his forearm to Tim. He **surveyed** him

20 narrowly, trying to decide how to respond. Tim looked at Ox in admiration and smiled. "Look, man," Tim said, "I don't want to bust you. I just want in."

Ox jerked his head toward the gym owner, Paul. "Don't talk to me. Talk to him. He's got the stuff. It'll cost you plenty, but I will say this—that's so-o-ome juice that dude has."

biceps *(adjective)*
a muscle in the upper arm

steroids *(noun)*
compounds that help to control body systems

1. Why is Tim discouraged?

   _____

   _____

2. Do you think Tim will start taking steroids? What do you think the results will be?

   _____

   _____

Highlight or underline what happens after Tim starts taking the steroids.

25   Without another thought, Tim walked over to Paul, who was sitting in his office, surrounded by pictures of weightlifting **icons.** He looked up when Tim came in and motioned him to a chair.

   "Hey," Tim said. "I'm looking for some of the juice you get for Ox. Works for him, huh?"

30   Paul cracked a smile. "You could say that. I've got some good stuff. It'll cost you, but it's worth it. Turns jelly to muscle like that." Paul snapped his fingers. "You start taking these babies, and you'll see something happen in weeks, not months."

   Tim nodded, trying to look unexcited, but he was **ecstatic.** This was what
35 he wanted. Not just working hard, but having something to show for it. Paul named a sum. Tim was a little surprised at how high it was, even though Paul had warned him. But he handed over the cash and pocketed the pills.

   It might have been Tim's overeager imagination, or because he wanted the steroids to work so badly, but within weeks, he felt his muscles grow. He could
40 lift more, and his body looked sculpted . He loved the moment every day when he popped those babies into his mouth. One day, Ox walked by while Tim was bench-pressing a considerable amount of weight. Ox grunted.

   "That juice is working for you," he said as he strode by, nodding in Tim's direction. Tim grunted back, but **inwardly,** he beamed.

45   Spending time in the gym became even more of an **obsession** with Tim. He would work out every day, sometimes twice a day. It was all he could think about. Sometimes he found himself stroking his biceps in the mirror at home. Once his girlfriend Meg caught him at it and made fun of him. She didn't think much of his growing gym habit, but even she admitted that the results
50 were impressive.

3. Why does Ox say the juice is working for Tim?

   _____

   _____

sculpted (adjective)
   cut into a desired shape

4. How can you tell working out has become an obsession for Tim?

_____

_____

Tim has the muscles he wanted. What do you think will happen next? Place an arrow in the margin when you find out.

As Tim spent more and more time in the gym, and less time with Meg, she started complaining. "Enough, already," she whined as he headed out for his second session of the day. "You look great, but what's the point of looking good if you're never out where anybody can see you?"

55   Tim snapped. "Would you get off my back?" he spat out. "It's my life, not yours."

"And you're not yourself any more," she yelled back "Don't bother coming back here. I don't want whatever it is you've turned into!" She slammed the door after him.

60   Tim found himself in an **unaccountable** fury. For the first time, he understood the meaning of the phrase to "see red." His vision clouded with a kind of red mist. He slammed his fist against the apartment wall, and it punched through. He looked at his fist in surprise.

At the gym, he told Ox what had happened. He and Ox had gotten close.
65   " Roid rage ," Ox said. "It happens. Like those pimples on your face."

"What are you talking about?" Tim yelled, although he knew the acne on his face had sprouted since he had started on the juice. "I ought to break your stupid neck!"

"Whoa, baby, you got it bad," Ox said, his palms up, backing off with a
70   **smirk** on his face. "You oughta lay off the juice."

Tim found his face **contorting** into an angry scowl. "Lay off," he snarled.

"Dude!" Ox said. "Look at yourself! Acne. Rage. Those are classic steroid symptoms. You need to think about what you're doing."

Tim opened his mouth to say something. Then he shut it. He thought
75   about what happened with Meg, the rage that seemed to come from nowhere, the acne. Maybe, he mused, maybe I do need to rethink the steroids.

roid rage (noun)
the anger that steroid use can cause

5. What is Meg's reaction to the time Tim spends in the gym?

_____

_____

6. Why does Ox tell Tim he needs to think about what he's doing?

_____

_____

After You Read

Build a robust vocabulary.

Writing Sentences   Write a complete sentence to respond to each of the following questions or statements. Use the underlined word in your answer. Use the definitions on page 5 to help you.

1. Who are two of the best-known sports <u>icons</u> of today?

   _____

2. Name something you have had an <u>obsession</u> about.

   _____

3. Tell about the last time you were <u>ecstatic</u>.

   _____

4. What is something you do <u>faithfully</u>?

   _____

5. If you are <u>contorting</u> your face, what does it look like?

   _____

Sentence Completions   Complete each sentence using a word from the box.

contorting	ecstatic	faithfully	icons	inwardly
obsession	smirk	specimens	surveyed	unaccountable

1. There was a _____ on Ed's face when he came in first place.

2. Those guys are strong physical _____ who show how working out changes your life.

3. His yelling at me was an _____ action, since I hadn't said a word to him.

4. The man at the party _____ the food table to see if there were any hamburgers.

5. Mack told Sandy he loved her dress, but _____ he thought it looked terrible on her.

Word Building   When an action happened in the past, you often add *-ed* to the end of the verb, the action word. For example, the word *paint* becomes *painted*. If there is an *e* on the end of the verb, you add only the *-d*, as in *embrace* and *embraced*. If the last syllable of the verb has a short vowel, you usually double the last consonant. *Drop* becomes *dropped*.

Change each of the verbs below to its past form. Then write a sentence using the past form.

1. surprise: _____

_____

2. wave: _____

_____

3. visit: _____

_____

4. clap: _____

_____

5. miss: _____

_____

TIP: Not every past tense verb is formed by adding *-ed*. Sometimes there is no pattern. You just have to know the word. What is the past form of *cut?* It's *cut.* What is the past form of *fly?* It's *flew.*

Writing Activity   Write a short paragraph that correctly uses key vocabulary words to tell what Tim experienced at the gym. Use at least four of the words from the list on page 5. Reread the definitions, if necessary.

_____

_____

_____

Think about your reading.

Check your comprehension.   Answer each question. If you don't know the answer, reread the lines in parentheses.

1. Why does Tim decide to talk to Ox? (lines 10–13)

_____

2. What happens soon after Tim begins to take the steroids? (lines 38–40)

_____

3. What symptoms of steroid use does Ox point out to Tim? (line 65)

_____

4. Why does Tim begin to think Ox is right that he shouldn't continue taking the steroids? (lines 74–76)

_____

Use reading skills: Make inferences.

You **make inferences** while you are reading, often without thinking about it. For example, if you read "George heard the smoke alarm shriek," you make the inference that there is a fire. When you make an inference, you add what is in the reading to what you know. You know why a smoke alarm goes off, so the inference you make is that there is a fire.

Make inferences. Write an inference about the sentences from the story.

> "Yeah," thought Tim, "and unless I'm an idiot, he's buying those muscles by popping steroids."

1. Inference: _____

   _____

> Paul snapped his fingers. "You start taking these babies, and you'll see something happen in weeks, not months."

2. Inference: _____

   _____

Use a graphic organizer.

Complete these graphic organizers to make inferences about the story.

What You Read	What You Know
Sometimes, he found himself stroking his biceps in the mirror at home.	1.

Inference You Make
2.

What You Read	What You Know
He slammed his fist against the apartment wall, and it punched through. He looked at his fist in surprise.	3.

Inference You Make
4.

Write about it.

Write a letter to the editor.

A letter to the editor may be an opinion about something or someone in the news. Imagine that you are Tim's friend and you are writing a letter to tell people what happened to Tim. You want to warn people of the dangers of using steroids in recreational sports. You'll need to give your view and use details and examples to back up your point of view.

Prewriting   The main idea of the letter is to tell people about the dangers of using steroids. You can use this idea web to help you write down the points you want to cover in your letter. First explain how you feel about steroids in recreational sports. Write your opinion in the large center oval. Then write the details, facts, and examples that back up your point of view in the other ovals.

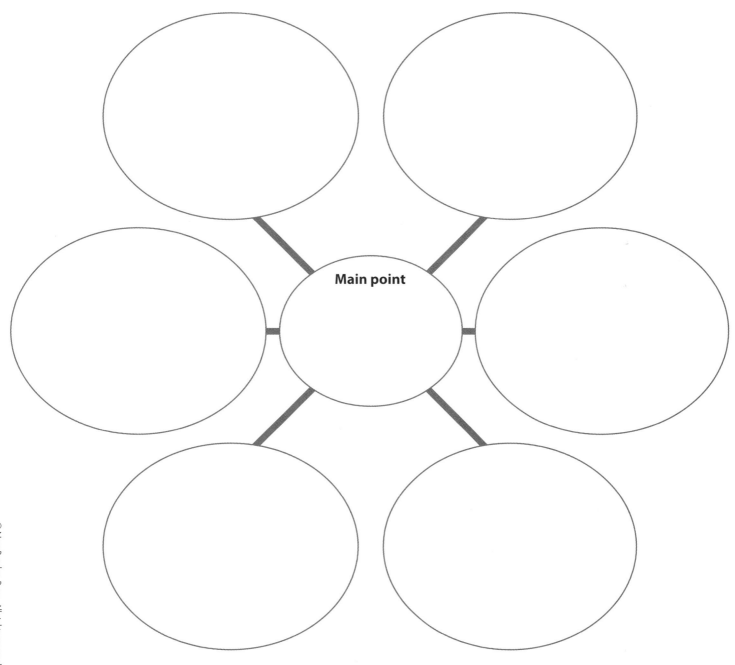

Thinking Beyond Reading   Think about these questions and discuss them with a partner. Add ideas to the graphic organizer as you talk.

- What did you learn about steroid use from reading the story?

- Is there ever a good reason to use steroids in sports?

- Should steroids be allowed in recreational sports? In professional sports?

- Why shouldn't an athlete be able to decide for himself or herself whether or not to use steroids?

Write a draft.   On a separate piece of paper, write a first draft of your letter to the editor. Follow the form of a business letter, writing the heading, the body of the letter, and the closing.

If you are against steroid use, your letter might begin: "Steroids should be banned from recreational sports because they give an unfair advantage and also carry health risks." As you write, try to imagine the person reading the letter. Use the details in your web to help you organize your ideas. Make your letter as clear and as specific as you can.

Your name
Your address
Date

Newspaper's name
Newspaper's address

Dear Editor:

Body of letter

Sincerely,
Your signature
Your name

Revise and create a final draft.   Write your final draft on a separate piece of paper. As you revise, check your draft for these specific points:

- Does your letter to the editor have a clear main point?

- Does your letter have details and examples that back up that main point?

- Did you follow standard business letter form?

- Did you check spelling and grammar to make sure your writing is clear and correct?

On the Job

Learning Objectives

In this lesson you will:

▨ Read a story about a man's problem at work.

▨ Make judgments about the people in the story.

▨ Master the key vocabulary used in the story.

▨ Write an opinion paragraph about what a company should do about a worker who may be stealing.

Key Vocabulary

condone *(verb)* to pardon or overlook; to treat as if not important

confronted *(verb)* challenged

dilemma *(noun)* a difficult choice

engulfing *(verb)* flooding or overwhelming

jeopardize *(verb)* to expose to danger or risk

lethargic *(adjective)* without energy

recite *(verb)* to repeat something that you have memorized

sauntered *(verb)* walked slowly and casually; strolled

surreptitiously *(adverb)* secretly

threadbare *(adjective)* worn; shabby

Before You Read

The man in the following story is a waiter in a restaurant. As you begin to read this story, visualize what the restaurant looks like and what the man does as he serves diners. Visualizing is an active reading strategy that will help you understand the story better.

Use what you know.

1. What kinds of jobs have you had?

   _____

   _____

   _____

2. Have you ever had a problem at your job? Explain.

   _____

   _____

   _____

3. What, if anything, did you do to resolve the work problem?

   _____

   _____

   _____

THINK ABOUT IT

I had a job working in a fast food burger place. It was hot in the back and I had to work fast. I liked the people I worked with, except for my boss, who was always yelling. Two months later I got a better job with a boss who was calmer.

Make predictions.

1. Read the title of the story. What does it say about the characters in the story? What does the picture suggest?

   _____

   _____

   _____

2. Read the first three paragraphs of the story. What is Richard worried about? What do you think will happen?

   _____

   _____

   _____

THINK ABOUT IT

Richard seems to be worried about Marco. I wonder why.

Among Friends

Read the following story to find out what happens to two waiters at work. In the margins, draw or jot down notes about what you see in your head as you read.

Richard came home from a long day of work at the restaurant. He was **lethargic.** His legs ached and his head throbbed. He removed his work shoes and leaned back on the **threadbare** couch.

"What's wrong, honey?" asked his wife. "You look tired. No tips today?"

5   "Tips were OK," Richard said. "It's Marco. There's something going on."

Richard and Marco, both 23, had been friends since childhood. Growing up, they lived in the same building and had gone to the same public schools. They were such good friends that they were even each other's best man at their weddings.

"He's rude to the customers. Today he cursed at one of them under his breath.
10 He seems angry. If he doesn't change his attitude, he's going to get fired."

"Talk to him, babe," said his wife. "Find out what's going on."

The next day was a Saturday, the busiest night at Il Postino. Richard drove his old battered Honda to work, parking in the lot behind the bistro . He got there early, hoping to speak to his friend before setup. But Marco hadn't arrived
15 yet, so Richard began to work along with four other waiters.

First, they took down the chairs from the tops of the tables and set them on the floor. Then they entered the kitchen to get the tablecloths and cutlery , which they used to set the tables. Then they placed a bouquet of wildflowers, a pitcher of ice water, as well as salt and pepper shakers, in the middle of each table.

20   "Tonight's specials are Homemade Pasta stuffed with ground beef and peppers, and Blackened Fresh Snapper," said Gustavo, the head waiter, as he prepped the waiters for the evening meal.

Every so often, Richard heard steps at the door, and he glanced up to see if Marco had come in.

25   "Where's Marco?" Mr. Puccio, the owner, demanded. "He's late—again!" the owner said, scowling. Clearly, Mr. Puccio was annoyed and Richard understood why.

"He'll be here soon," said Richard.

bistro *(noun)*
  a small, casual restaurant

cutlery *(noun)*
  implements for cutting or eating food

specials *(noun)*
  featured dishes at a restaurant

prepped *(verb)*
  prepared

Marco had gotten Richard the job, so Richard felt it was his responsibility to help his friend, if he could.

30 Finally, Marco **sauntered** in. His expression spelled trouble.

"Hey, man," Richard whispered to his friend. "What's up? You're late. The boss is plenty upset."

"Nothing," said Marco. "Get off my back."

1. What was bothering Richard after work?

_____

_____

2. How did Richard show he is a good friend of Marco's?

_____

_____

Continue reading the story to find out how Marco surprised Richard. In the margins, draw small pictures to show how you picture the main events.

Soon the restaurant filled with hungry, excited customers, **engulfing** the
35 room with conversation and laughter. Richard and Marco had no time to talk. They were busy taking dinner orders, walking back and forth through the swinging kitchen doors, carrying trays, serving meals, and totaling bills.

"Have a nice evening," said Richard to a customer. Then he approached the corner of the room where a tip box was resting on a round, wooden table. It was
40 there the waiters deposited the tips for the day. At Il Postino, all six waiters pooled their tips every evening, rather than keeping their tips individually. As he came closer to the table, Richard noticed Marco standing over it, with his back to the dining room. To Richard's horror, he saw Marco pull out two ten dollar bills and stuff them **surreptitiously** into his pants pocket.

45 Richard was shocked, and mad, and confused. This was a friend he had known since kindergarten. They had watched each other's backs for all these years. Now he saw Marco in a different light. The guy was a thief, robbing him—Richard— and all the other waiters who trusted him. After all, they depended on each other's honesty. If one man stole from the tip box, the others suffered.

50 "What are you doing?" demanded Richard. "You could get fired for that!"

"Huh?" asked Marco, pretending innocence.

"I saw what you did. That's for all of us, not just you. It's not your personal piggy bank."

"Forget what you saw. I'll pay you later," Marco replied. Enraged, Marco
55 charged back to the dining room.

What should he do? thought Richard. If he reported what he saw to Mr. Puccio, Marco could get fired. If he told the other waiters, he'd risk Marco's physical safety. But he just couldn't **condone** Marco's behavior.

And what if this wasn't the first or only time Marco stole? If he stole before,
60 then Marco owed all the guys even more money. Richard was torn, didn't know what to think or what action to take. Clearly, Richard faced a **dilemma.**

3. Do you think Richard had a right to be angry at Marco? Explain.

_____

_____

4. What do you think Richard should do about Marco's actions? Why?

_____

_____

Finish reading the story to find out how the friendship between Richard and Marco changes. In your mind, picture the two men talking in the parking lot.

After work that night, Richard **confronted** Marco in the parking lot.

"We're talking now, whether you like it or not," said Richard, shoving his friend on to the hood of his car. "What's happening?"

65 "I can't take it anymore," said Marco angrily. "The long hours. The heavy trays. The picky customers. Work on weekends and holidays. And for what? These low wages? I'm fed up. I'm mad. I'm gonna quit or get fired. One or the other."

"Quit? Are you crazy?" said Richard, furious. "Get another job, but don't **jeopardize** your reputation, your honor, by stealing! Go out with your head held

70 high, not like a crook. If you get caught, get fired, where will you be? You'll never find a better job. You'll need references ."

Marco stared at the ground, thinking. He looked stricken with the foolishness of his recent behavior. The next day, Marco called in sick. Then he took a week off for personal days. When he came back eight days later, he looked relaxed and relieved.

75 "I gave notice," grinned Marco. "I'm the new head waiter at Café Carmelo, down the block. I start in two weeks," said Marco. "Pay increase. Better hours. And this is for you and the guys." He handed Richard three ten dollar bills.

"I owe you guys $20, plus $10 to you for the good advice. And for being a pal," said Marco. "And if you ever want to change jobs, come see me at Café Carmelo."

80 "No way," said Richard. "I would never work with a guy like you."

"Aw, c'mon, man," Marco replied.

"You heard me. How do I know if you stole from us before? Just remember, Marco, what goes around, comes around. Put the $20 in the box and keep the extra $10. And don't come near me; I need to cool down. I've got to think things

85 over. Until then, keep away."

And with that, Richard turned, approaching table four to **recite** to a hungry family of six the special entrees for the night.

references *(noun)*
statements about the qualities of a person applying for a job

entrees *(noun)*
main courses

5. What has Marco done to hurt Richard and the other waiters?

_____

_____

6. What would you have done about Marco if you were Richard? Explain.

_____

_____

After You Read

Build a robust vocabulary.

Writing Sentences   Write a complete sentence to respond to each of the following questions or statements. Use the underlined word in your answer. Use the definitions on page 15 to help you.

1.   Tell about a time when you felt <u>lethargic</u>.

   _____

2.   Name something that might be <u>threadbare</u>.

   _____

3.   Tell about a time you <u>confronted</u> someone.

   _____

4.   Tell about a <u>dilemma</u> you had at home, school, or work.

   _____

5.   Can you <u>recite</u> all the words to the Pledge of Allegiance?

   _____

Sentence Completions   Complete each sentence using a word from the box.

condone	**confronted**	**dilemma**	**engulfing**	**jeopardize**
lethargic	**recite**	**sauntered**	**surreptitiously**	**threadbare**

1.   The sound of the band was _____ the small room.

2.   It's best not to _____ your job by doing something wrong.

3.   He hid the money _____ under his shirt.

4.   Raul _____ into the meeting 30 minutes late.

5.   Would you _____ the behavior of a good friend who stole from you?

Word Building   Many **plural** nouns are formed just by adding -*s* or -*es*. You make some nouns plural in a special way. With words that end in *f* or *fe*, you change the *f* to *v* before adding -*s* or -*es*. For example, the plural of *leaf* is *leaves*. The plural of *wife* is *wives*.

Change each of the nouns below to its plural form. Then write a sentence using the plural.

1. knife: _____

_____

2. loaf: _____

_____

3. half: _____

_____

4. calf: _____

_____

5. wharf: _____

_____

TIP: Not every word that ends in -s is a plural. You need to read the words around a word to see if it has to do with more than one thing. For example, the word *glass* ends in an *s* but is not a plural. *Glasses* is the plural form of *glass*.

Writing Activity   Write a short paragraph that correctly uses key vocabulary words to tell about a job you have or had. Use at least four of the words from the list on page 15. Reread the definitions, if necessary.

_____

_____

_____

Think about your reading.

Check your comprehension.   Answer each question. If you don't know the answer, reread the lines in parentheses.

1. What did Richard and Marco have in common from the past? (lines 6–8)

_____

2. In what ways did Richard show he was a good friend to Marco? (lines 27–32)

_____

3. How could Marco have handled his anger better at work? (lines 68–70)

_____

4. Will Richard ever go to Marco to find a better job? (line 80)

_____

Use reading skills: Make judgments.

As you read, you **make judgments** about the actions of the people in an article or story by combining what the author or characters said or did with your own experience.

Make judgments. Reread the following paragraph from the story. Then write the answers to the questions.

> Then Richard approached the corner of the room where a tip box was resting on a round, wooden table. It was there the waiters deposited the tips for the day. At Il Postino, all six waiters pooled their tips every evening, rather than keeping their tips individually. As he came closer to the table, Richard noticed Marco standing over it, with his back to the dining room. To Richard's horror, he saw Marco pull out two ten dollar bills and stuff them surreptitiously into his pants pocket.

1. What did Richard see Marco do?

   _____

2. What is your judgment about Marco's character?

   _____

Use a graphic organizer.

Here is a graphic organizer that helps you make a judgment. In the table below, fill in the sentence that tells what judgment you made based on the story and what you know. Use the ideas in the story and your own.

The story says	Marco stole money from the tip box.
I know	Friends don't steal from each other.
My judgment	

Write about it.

Write an opinion paragraph.

In opinion writing you express your viewpoint on a subject. You state both sides of an issue, then tell which side you favor and why.

Imagine that you work in the Human Resources department of a large chain of restaurants. Jack, a longtime waiter at one restaurant, has been accused by the cook of stealing two steaks from the kitchen. Over the years, Jack has brought in many customers because of his prompt service and his friendly personality with the customers. Your supervisor asks for your judgment of what to do about Jack.

Prewriting   On your own or with a partner, jot down ideas the paragraph will include. Explain what the issue is, describe Jack's value to the company over the years, tell what you think the company should do about the accusation, and give reasons for your judgment. Fill in the graphic organizer with your ideas. Add more supporting details, if you like.

The facts say	Jack has been accused of stealing steaks from the kitchen.
I know	
My judgment	

Thinking Beyond Reading   Think about these questions and discuss them with a partner. Add ideas to the graphic organizer as you talk.

- Have you ever known anyone falsely accused of something? Explain.

- What proof is there of Jack's theft?

- What are some good reasons to speak to Jack about the accusation?

- What action is best for the restaurant?

- What action is best for Jack?

Write a draft.   Write a first draft of your opinion paragraph. You might begin with the following sentence: "Jack was accused of stealing two steaks from the restaurant last Thursday." Explain the different alternatives the restaurant has. State your judgment about what the restaurant should do.

_____

_____

_____

_____

_____

_____

_____

_____

_____

_____

_____

_____

Revise and create a final draft.   Write your final draft on a separate piece of paper. As you revise, check your draft for these specific points.

- Did you state the situation?

- Did you explain the alternatives the restaurant has?

- Did you state your judgment about what the restaurant should do?

- Did you check spelling and grammar to make sure your writing is clear and correct?

We Are Family

Learning Objectives

In this lesson you will:

▨ Learn about families with only one child.

▨ Synthesize information.

▨ Master the key vocabulary used in the article.

▨ Write an explanation.

Key Vocabulary

aggravations *(noun)* irritations

anxiety *(noun)* feeling of being worried that something bad will happen

emotionally *(adverb)* with strong feelings

extensive *(adjective)* wide in range

financially *(adverb)* related to money

resolve *(verb)* to deal with something successfully, to clear up

socializing *(verb)* associating with others

status *(noun)* a person's position in relation to others

stigma *(noun)* a mark of shame

unique *(adjective)* distinctively characteristic

Before You Read

See if you can find one or two active reading strategies that work best for you. Try using what you know. In this article you'll learn why there are more only children in this country than there used to be. Think about your own experience growing up with or without brothers and sisters.

Here's another effective active reading strategy you can try. Ask yourself questions as you read. This will keep you focused on the story and make it easier for you to understand what you are reading.

Use what you know.

1. How many brothers and sisters did you have growing up?

   _____

   _____

   _____

2. What did you like about having or not having brothers or sisters?

   _____

   _____

   _____

3. What did you dislike about having or not having brothers or sisters?

   _____

   _____

   _____

Ask yourself questions.

1. Why might parents decide to have only one child?

   _____

   _____

   _____

2. Are there advantages or disadvantages to being an only child?

   _____

   _____

   _____

The Only Child

Read the following article to find out how the lives of only children differ from those of children with brothers and sisters. Highlight or underline phrases that show how the lives of only children are different.

When you were growing up, did you share toys with your younger brother? Argue with your older sister? Did you tell each other scary stories at nighttime? If your family was like many families in America, you grew up, for better or worse, in a household with other children.

5 But in the last few years, more children are being raised as the only child in the home. With no brothers or sisters, these children have **unique** experiences. At the dinner table, they are the only ones with child-sized plates. When it comes to dessert, there's no need to argue over which kid gets the bigger slice of pie. After dinner, they play by themselves.

10 Experts wonder many things about only children and their families. For one, they wonder why the number of only-child households is growing. Second they wonder if adult onlies turn out differently from those with siblings. Experts conducted studies about these issues, and the results are fascinating.

Mine! All Mine!

15 The number of households with only children has increased greatly. In fact, it has doubled in the last 30 years. In the late 1970s, for example, less than ten percent of women ages 40 to 44 had an only child. But in 2004, over 17 percent had an only.

Says a 42-year-old woman with one child, "When I was growing up, I had three sisters. We had fun playing outside, but we also fought a lot. It's different for 20 my son. He doesn't fight with anyone, but he also plays by himself."

Today there are 14 million only children in America. Let's look at the three main reasons why that number is growing every year.

onlies (noun)
children who have no brothers or sisters

siblings (noun)
brothers and sisters

1. What is one question experts wondered about only children?

_____

_____

2. Over the last 30 years, how has the number of only children changed?

_____

_____

Continue reading to find out *why* the number of families with only children is growing. Draw a star beside each paragraph that gives a reason.

You Go Your Way . . .

The main reason for smaller families is the increased divorce rate. Years ago,
25 parents stayed together for life, but today, 50 percent of married couples break up. As families divorce, there are fewer babies born. Reports one California woman, "When my ex and I went our separate ways, neither of us remarried. So we had our one son, and that was that."

The Economy

30 The second reason for the trend is related to inflation . With the cost of food and clothing on the rise, parents realize that the more children they have, the more expensive it will be to raise them. Also, parents see that the more money they spend on their children, the less they have for the family as a whole. Many parents decide, therefore, to limit the number of children in order to have greater
35 financial resources.

A Difficult Juggling Act

There is a third reason for the trend toward one-child families. In the 1950s, many women stayed home and cared for their children. But today more women are employed outside the home. These women are involved with their jobs and
40 have less time and energy to care for the children. Women realize that it's difficult to juggle the demands of parenthood with those of a job. "I work a 10-hour day, five days a week," says a mother of a six-year-old. "It's hard enough taking care of my daughter. If I had a second kid, I don't know how I'd handle it physically, **emotionally,** or **financially."**

45 ### How Do Only Children Turn Out?

Many researchers wonder how the lives of only children differ from those of children with siblings. Are only children more verbal, less verbal, or the same? Are onlies as good at **socializing** as children raised with other kids? And, do only children grow up to be as happy as kids with sibs?
50 To find out the answers to these questions, scientists conducted studies. They looked at the test scores of only children and compared them with the scores of children with siblings. They also observed children from both groups and asked parents about their children's moods and behaviors.

inflation *(noun)*
a continuing
rise in prices

The results of these studies are interesting. Overall, they found that once only children reach adulthood, there is little difference between them and those with siblings. Only children do just fine. Experts did find that the verbal abilities of only children were more **extensive.** But they also found that by the time children of both groups turned 25, their vocabularies were about the same.

3. Why are there more only children now than there used to be?

_____

_____

4. What are the differences between only children and children with siblings?

_____

_____

Finish reading the article to find out whether onlies are as happy as other adults. Highlight or underline the sentences that give you that information.

More Results

Are only kids as happy as those raised with other kids? In general, they are. But some only children suffer from what's known as "only-child **stigma.**" Said one seven-year-old, "Kids at school keep asking me why I don't have a brother or sister. I tell them I have two cats and a bird and that's good enough for me." Observed two writers who specialize in only children, "Sibling **status** has little to do with determining happiness."

"For every only child who wishes she had a sibling," the writers observed, "there is an angry teen who complains about her bratty younger brother. In short, the lives of onlies are filled with the same joys and **aggravations** as those with siblings."

Sometimes it's not the only child who feels unhappy, but the parents of that child who feel that way. Parents worry that their only child may feel lonely. How do some parents **resolve** that? Some take the child to day care, where he or she interacts with other kids. Or they involve the child in sports teams or play-dates with cousins, neighbors, or friends. Some sign the child up for classes. These activities seem to help children socialize and relieve parents' **anxiety.**

Regardless of what the experts say, one Texas man, now in his 50s, describes his early years this way. "I loved being an only kid. I was the boss of my trucks, the TV, and my dog. Who wouldn't want to grow up like that?"

5. Describe the stigma some only children suffer from as kids.

_____

_____

6. What are some advantages and disadvantages of being an only child?

_____

_____

After You Read

Build a robust vocabulary.

Writing Sentences   Write a complete sentence to respond to each of the following questions or statements. Use the underlined word in your answer. Use the definitions on page 25 to help you.

1.   Tell about a time you felt <u>anxiety</u>.

   _____

2.   What can a person do to become <u>financially</u> secure?

   _____

3.   Explain one way in which you are <u>unique</u> in your family.

   _____

4.   Tell about a time you reacted <u>emotionally</u>.

   _____

5.   What are some <u>aggravations</u> in your life?

   _____

Sentence Completions   Complete each sentence using a word from the box.

aggravations	anxiety	emotionally	extensive	financially
resolve	socializing	status	stigma	unique

1.   Tammy was pleased with her _____ as the oldest daughter.

2.   Pat's understanding of economics is _____.

3.   How did Rosa _____ the problem at her job?

4.   On weekends Betty is usually _____ with her friends at the community center.

5.   Ruby didn't feel that there was a _____ attached to being an only child.

Word Building   A **root word** is the main part of a word that contains its basic meaning. For example, the word *social* is the root word in *socializing.* The suffix (ending) *-izing* was added to the root word.

Circle the root word in each word below. Then write another word that uses the same root word, but has a different prefix or suffix. Then write a sentence using the new word.

1. adjustment: _____

   _____

2. frustration: _____

   _____

3. unlikely: _____

   _____

4. visitor: _____

   _____

5. presentation: _____

   _____

TIP: When you read, you may find some words you do not know. Think, "What is the root of the word? What does the root mean? How does the prefix or suffix change the meaning of the word?"

Writing Activity Write a short paragraph that correctly uses key vocabulary words to tell about how the parent of an only child may feel about having one child. Use at least four of the words from the list on page 25. Reread the definitions, if necessary.

_____

_____

_____

Think about your reading.

Check your comprehension. Answer each question. If you don't know the answer, reread the lines in parentheses.

1. What percent of American women ages 40–44 in 2004 had an only child? (line 17)

   _____

2. What is a major reason for the increased number of only children in the United States? (lines 24–26)

   _____

3. Compare the happiness of adult onlies with people raised with siblings. (lines 64–67)

   _____

4. Why do parents of onlies often worry about their kids? (line 69)

   _____

Use reading skills: Synthesize information.

When you **synthesize,** you take parts of what you read and put them together to reach a new understanding. For example, you might read about how to bathe a dog, feed a dog, and walk a dog. You could then synthesize that information to explain how to be a good dog owner.

Synthesize information. As you read "The Only Child," you probably synthesized ideas many times.

Reread the following paragraph from the article.

> Sometimes it's not the only child who feels unhappy, but the parents of that child who feel that way. Parents worry that their only child may feel lonely. How do some parents resolve that? Some take the child to day care, where he or she interacts with other kids. Or they involve the child in sports teams or play-dates with cousins, neighbors, or friends. Some sign the child up for classes. These activities seem to help children socialize and relieve parents' anxiety.

1. What does the paragraph say about why some parents of only children are unhappy?

    _____

2. What do they do to relieve their concerns?

    _____

3. What can you synthesize from these two pieces of information?

    _____

Use a graphic organizer.

You can use a graphic organizer like the one below to help you synthesize information. In the boxes on top, write different things parents of only children do to relieve their anxiety. The first box is filled in for you. What can you synthesize from this information?

1. They take their children to daycare.	2.	3.

↓

Synthesize the information

Write about it.

Write an explanation.

Your neighbor is worried about her daughter, an only child. Caroline, age eight, has few kids to play with after school, though sometimes she plays with Jenny, your nine-year-old daughter. Write a note to your neighbor suggesting how Caroline can socialize with others and learn new skills. Suggest some activities that might help her make friends.

Prewriting   On your own or with a partner, write the ideas that you will include in your explanation. Use information from the article along with your own ideas. Fill in the graphic organizer with your ideas.

What I read	What I know	Suggestions and benefits
1. Some parents sign up their child for classes.	My sister's daughter took dance classes. Now she is best friends with one of the girls in her class.	Enroll Caroline in an after-school dance class. It will be good exercise and a good social experience for her.
2. Some parents arrange play dates for their child.		
3. Some parents involve their child in sports.		

Thinking Beyond Reading   Think about these questions and discuss them with a partner. Add ideas to the graphic organizer as you talk.

- In your experience, what kinds of after-school activities do eight-year-old girls like to do?

- What kinds of activities might there be at a local community center?

- What other benefits are there to these activities?

- How do you think Caroline and her mother will feel if Caroline socializes with other kids?

Write a draft.   Write a first draft of your explanation. Your explanation might begin with this sentence: "Caroline can engage in many after-school and weekend activities at the community center." Use the ideas in your chart to help you complete your explanation.

_____

_____

_____

_____

_____

_____

_____

_____

_____

_____

_____

_____

_____

_____

_____

Revise and create a final draft.   Write your final draft on a separate piece of paper. As you revise, check your draft for these specific points.

- Did you write a topic sentence that sums up the main point of the paragraph?

- Does your explanation give three clear suggestions for how Caroline's mother can get her daughter actively involved in activities?

- Did you check spelling and grammar to make sure your writing is clear and correct?

Making a Comeback

Learning Objectives

In this lesson you will:

▓ Learn about a community that has gone through many changes.

▓ Identify main idea and details.

▓ Master the key vocabulary used in the article.

▓ Write a personal narrative about something that happened in your community.

Key Vocabulary

abandoned *(adjective)* deserted or given up

complex *(noun)* a structure made up of several connected parts

dependent *(adjective)* needing the help or presence of another

energize *(verb)* to make lively or active

experimental *(adjective)* using ideas not tried before

flourished *(verb)* achieved success

patriotic *(adjective)* inspired by love of one's country

revenue *(noun)* income

scarce *(adjective)* not plentiful

thriving *(verb)* growing well

Before You Read

The passage you are about to read is about a town that went through many changes over many years. After you read the title and the first paragraph, think about what you know about towns or cities. Then think about what you want to learn from reading the article.

Use what you know.

THINK ABOUT IT

1. What kind of community do you live in?

   _____

   _____

   _____

I live in Los Angeles. It's got a lot of traffic and noise. I notice that a lot of young kids are moving here to get jobs in the movies. Older families are moving out.

2. How has your community changed since you've lived there?

   _____

   _____

   _____

3. What kinds of changes would make your community better?

   _____

   _____

   _____

Set a purpose for reading.

THINK ABOUT IT

1. What can I learn from reading about North Adams?

   _____

   _____

   _____

I'd like to learn why the story of one particular town is important.

2. Why would the town have to change many times?

   _____

   _____

   _____

North Adams, Here We Come

Read the following article to find out how a town called North Adams, Massachusetts, made an economic comeback after going through hard times. Jot down your purpose for reading the article.

Have you ever gone through hard times, only to bounce back months or years later? Towns do that, too.

One town that experienced that kind of dramatic change is North Adams, Massachusetts. During the 1980s, it was economically depressed . Businesses had closed. People were unemployed. Residents moved to other cities to find jobs. Buildings were empty. Many thought North Adams was dying.

But in the late 1990s, the town became revitalized . New businesses opened. Men and women found jobs. People rented apartments again. Others bought houses. Once-empty buildings were cleaned up and the whole town was **thriving.**

What caused the change? Much of it can be credited to the opening in 1996 of a cultural center in the middle of town. The center was so unusual that people from all over the country wanted to attend events there, bringing in much needed **revenue.** Largely because of the center, the community of North Adams is growing once again.

Looking Back

North Adams, Massachusetts, is a town with an interesting history. Over the past 200 years, it has **flourished** or struggled, **dependent** on the rise or fall of businesses in one particular **complex** on Marshall Street.

From the late 1700s through the mid 1880s, North Adams was a mill town. The Hoosic River, which runs though the town, provided the waterpower to run the looms and other machines inside the huge, red-brick buildings. Businesses manufactured cloth, shoes, cabinets, hats, bricks, and works of marble. Jobs were easy to come by, as people were needed to operate the machines from early morning till late at night.

economically depressed
(adjective)
having very low business activity and income

revitalized *(adjective)*
full of new life

manufactured *(verb)*
made into a product suitable for use

1. Why were the activities on Marshall Street important to North Adams?

_____

_____

2. Why was the Hoosic River important to the mills during the 1800s?

_____

_____

Continue reading the article. Highlight or mark the sentences that tell what happened to North Adams when one company went out of business.

Times Change

25   In 1860, the Arnold Print Works moved into the building complex on Marshall Street. It became the country's leading manufacturer of printed cloth, so it needed lots of workers at the plant. By 1905, the plant provided jobs to more than 3,200 North Adams residents, who worked either the day or night shift.

    The Arnold Print Works plant was the central part of life in North Adams.
30 But it would not last. The Great Depression, a time of economic downturn, affected the entire country. Money became **scarce** and prices fell. So, in 1942, the Arnold Print Company downsized and moved away.

    Residents of North Adams were worried. Where would they find jobs? Would they have to move elsewhere to find work? They didn't want to. After all, many
35 men and women had been born in the town and had strong ties to their friends and neighbors. Besides, everything in North Adams was familiar and comfortable. With their main employer closing, what would happen to their town?

Sprague Lights Things Up

    Fortunately, the Sprague Electric Company was a booming business and it
40 was looking for a larger home. It found the former Arnold Print Works building suitable and moved in.

    Sprague added to the energy of the town in more ways than one. The electric company operated 24 hours a day, so workers came and left work at all hours. To encourage workers to support the country's involvement in World War II, the
45 company often played **patriotic** songs over loudspeakers. Sprague was a lively place.

    Sprague was also like a city within a city. It had its own radio station, day care center, sports teams, dances, orchestra, library, and vocational school.

    Sprague provided employment for almost one-fourth of the North Adams community. Nearly everyone in town had at least one family member working in
50 the complex. Often a Sprague worker found that the person on his or her left or right was a cousin, an uncle, or a sister.

    By the mid-1980s, times had changed. Electric parts could be produced more inexpensively in Asia. The Sprague business weakened. As a result, the company left North Adams in 1985.

55   The town faced troubled times again. Without jobs, people could no longer afford the mortgages or rent on their homes and apartments. Banks closed. Restaurants, dry cleaners, even funeral parlors closed as well. North Adams was going down.

economic downturn (noun)
decline in business or financial activity

downsized (verb)
reduced in size

mortgages (noun)
loans made to people to buy houses

3. How did the Great Depression affect the Arnold Print Works Company?

_____

_____

4. Was the Sprague Electric Company good for North Adams? Explain.

_____

_____

Finish reading the article to find out what happened to North Adams.

Many North Adams residents experienced a new kind of loss. With so many people leaving, those who remained lost the sense of closeness and community.
60 People felt less safe, and they were anxious about the future.

Bright Idea

Everyone wondered, "What can we do to **energize** North Adams once again? How can we bring back businesses and jobs to the area?" Then someone had a good idea. The huge, red brick buildings that were now empty might make an unusual
65 museum. The **abandoned** Sprague complex could house large art works that were too big to fit in smaller museums in major cities like New York or Boston.

People from all over the country might even travel long distances to see the art. But art wouldn't be the only thing to bring people there. There could be music and movies, too. In 1999, the museum known as MASS MoCA (the
70 Massachusetts Museum of Contemporary Art) opened its doors. On the first day, more than 50,000 people lined up to get in! Word spread that good things were happening in North Adams. The cultural center attracted more people.

Visitors needed places to eat, so new restaurants opened. Hotels opened too. Other types of businesses, such as technology and graphic design, found reasonable
75 rents there and set up shop.

Today, the museum in North Adams is known for its art. But it's also becoming famous for its Bang on a Can festival where musicians play or listen to rock, jazz, and **experimental** music.

North Adams isn't flourishing these days, but it is improving economically.
80 And the good features of the town have returned. Said one man, "The city doesn't have any money, but it's extremely rich." People, he said, are responsible toward each other. They check on their neighbors. "There's a sense of community here," he said. "And that's what counts."

5. Besides money, what else did the people of North Adams lose?

_____

_____

6. What turned things around for the town of North Adams?

_____

_____

After You Read

Build a robust vocabulary.

Writing Sentences   Write a complete sentence to respond to each of the following questions or statements. Use the underlined word in your answer. Use the definitions on page 35 to help you.

1. Name a person who is <u>dependent</u> on you or who you are dependent on.

   _____

2. If a baby is <u>thriving</u>, what would he be doing?

   _____

3. How can a person show she is <u>patriotic</u>?

   _____

4. Tell about a time when money was <u>scarce</u> in your life.

   _____

5. Describe an event that can <u>energize</u> a party.

   _____

Sentence Completions   Complete each sentence using a word from the box.

abandoned	complex	dependent	energize	experimental
flourished	patriotic	revenue	scarce	thriving

1. The old building was _____ last year.

2. Businesses lost _____ when they were flooded.

3. My brother _____ after he recovered from a long illness.

4. Jazz was once considered an _____ form of music.

5. We got lost when we walked through the large _____ of buildings.

Word Building Prefixes   A **prefix** is a group of letters added to the beginning of a word that changes its meaning. For example, the prefix *re-* means "again." The word *rewrite* means "to write again." Here are some other prefixes and their meanings.

Prefix	Meaning
mis-	bad, wrong
im-	not
un-	not

Read the words in the box. Circle the prefixes. Discuss with a partner what each word means.

| miscount | reopen | unbelievable | impossible |

Add the prefix *re-*, *mis-*, *im-*, or *un-* to the words in the sentences below. Use the context, or the words around the word, to tell which prefix to add.

1. The teacher hoped the children would not _____behave while she was out of the room.

2. The writer gave the movie an _____favorable review.

3. We asked our friend to _____tell the funny joke.

4. It is _____proper to talk while you're chewing food.

5. My friend is _____likely to be late.

TIP: You may be able to use what you know about prefixes to tell what a word you don't know means. For example, knowing the prefix *mis-* will help you understand that *mismanage* means "to manage badly."

Writing Activity   Write a short paragraph that correctly uses key vocabulary words to tell about a community in which you'd like to live. Use at least four of the words from the list on page 35. Reread the definitions, if necessary.

_____

_____

_____

_____

Think about your reading.

Check your comprehension.   Answer each question. If you don't know the answer, reread the lines in parentheses.

1. How did the closing of the Arnold Print Works affect the residents of the town? (lines 33–36)

_____

2. How did the Sprague Electric Company energize North Adams? (lines 42–50)

_____

3. How did North Adams change after the electric company closed? (lines 55–57)

_____

4. How did the new museum change the economic conditions in North Adams? (lines 71–75)

_____

Use reading skills: Identify main idea and details.

The **main idea** of an article tells what it is mostly about. This article is mostly about the changing economic conditions in North Adams, Massachusetts. **Supporting details** explain, describe, or give more information about the main idea. In this article each paragraph also has a main idea and details that support it.

Identify main idea and details. As you read "North Adams, Here We Come," you learned the main idea and supporting details about changes that took place in North Adams.

Reread the following paragraph from the article.

> Residents of North Adams were worried. Where would they find jobs? Would they have to move elsewhere to find work?

1. Write the sentence that tells the main idea of the paragraph.

    _____

2. Write the two details that support, or give reasons that explain, the main idea.

    _____

Use a graphic organizer.

Reread the following paragraph. Find the main idea and two supporting details in the paragraph. Write them in the graphic organizer below.

> Sprague added to the energy of the town in more ways than one. The electric company operated 24 hours a day, so workers came and left work at all hours. To encourage workers to support the country's involvement in World War II, the company often played patriotic songs over loudspeakers. Sprague was a lively place.

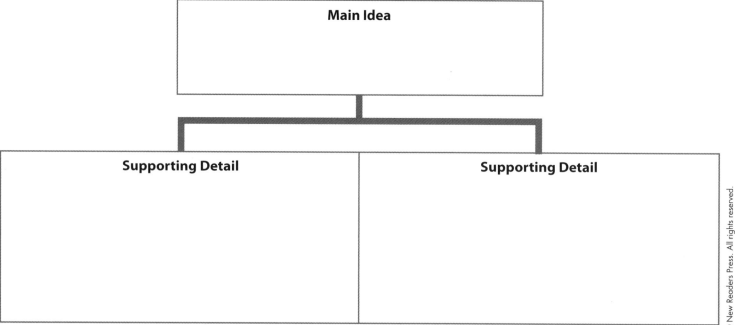

Main Idea

Supporting Detail   **Supporting Detail**

Write about it.

Write a personal narrative.

A personal narrative is the story of a specific event in your life. Think of a place in your city or town that is important to you. It can be a street corner, a building, a park, or someplace else. Write a personal narrative paragraph about something that happened to you or that you did there.

Begin by stating your main idea. Explain in general terms what happened and why it was important to you. Then tell where you were when the incident happened, and who was with you. In other words, give details of what happened. Finally, tell how the incident and place changed you, or how you feel when you pass that place today.

Prewriting   On your own or with a partner, write the main idea and supporting details that you will include in your personal narrative. Fill in the graphic organizer with your ideas. Use as many boxes as you need for supporting details.

Main Idea

Supporting Detail	Supporting Detail	Supporting Detail	Supporting Detail

Thinking Beyond Reading   Think about these questions and discuss them with a partner. Add ideas to the graphic organizer as you talk.

- What is the one big idea that you want the reader to get from your writing?

- Why is the place or event important to you?

- How has the incident changed you?

- Could anything like this ever happen again?

Write a draft.   Write a first draft of your personal narrative paragraph. Your paragraph might begin with a sentence like this: "I'll never forget the day when . . . ." Go on to provide the supporting details. Conclude your narrative with a final statement that sums up why the event or place is important to you today. Use the ideas in your chart to help you complete your paragraph.

_____

_____

_____

_____

_____

_____

_____

_____

_____

_____

_____

_____

_____

Revise and create a final draft.   Write your final draft on a separate piece of paper. As you revise, check your draft for these specific points.

- Did you write a topic sentence that gives the main idea of the paragraph?

- Did you include details that tell about the main idea?

- Did you check spelling and grammar to make sure your writing is clear and correct?

Summer Vacations

Learning Objectives

In this lesson you will:

Learn about summer camps for children.

Distinguish between fact and opinion.

Master the key vocabulary used in the article.

Write a description.

Key Vocabulary

acquire *(verb)* to develop or learn

bond *(verb)* to develop a special relationship with someone

cater *(verb)* to provide someone with something they need or want

conventional *(adjective)* usual

environmental *(adjective)* having to do with the land, water, and air in which people, animals, and plants live

exclusively *(adverb)* limited to

luau *(noun)* a Hawaiian feast

relish *(verb)* to enjoy something

routine *(noun)* the usual or normal way you do things

supportive *(adjective)* giving help or encouragement

Before You Read

The article you are about to read is about camps for kids. To get started, ask yourself this active reading question: What do I already know about camps and other summer experiences for kids?

Another effective active reading strategy is to ask yourself questions about the article. Ask questions before, during, or after reading to see if you get the meaning.

Use what you know.

1. What kinds of things do you like to do when you take a vacation or get away?

   _____

   _____

   _____

Last year I took a few days off from work and went to Seattle. I visited my sister and brother-in-law. We went to the top of the Space Needle and we drove into the mountains. The trip was a great change of pace.

2. Where do you go when you want to get away?

   _____

   _____

   _____

Ask yourself questions.

1. My nephew has trouble reading. Is there a special camp where he can go for the summer?

   _____

   _____

If my child wanted to go to summer camp, I wonder how I'd choose the right one.

2. Why is it important for kids to go to camp?

   _____

   _____

   _____

What Happens at Summer Camp?

Read the article to find out what kinds of summer camps there are and who goes to them. Write down your questions to see if the article answers them.

Imagine that you're a kid again. It's the start of summer. School's out. Your friends are away visiting relatives. It's too hot to play outside. You're bored.

But not for long. Because in a few days, you might be headed for summer camp. This is your chance to experience outdoor life by swimming, boating, and hiking
5   with children your own age. While there, you'll learn camping skills like how to row a boat or how to identify a type of tree. Depending on the camp, you may also learn to take and develop photographs, work with computer programs, or improve your math skills. For sure, you'll come away with new abilities and knowledge you can use both in and out of school.

10 Every summer, millions of youngsters as young as 5 and as old as 18 leave their families for a week or more, and head to the mountains or woods for vacation. In the process, these kids get a break from their everyday **routine, acquire** new skills, and make new friends.

Summer camps **cater** to different kinds of children with various interests. Some
15 teach foreign languages, such as Chinese. Others teach storytelling. Still others teach **environmental** studies. Some camps prepare children for the upcoming school year by practicing reading, writing, and math in a pleasant atmosphere, under a tree or by a pond.

Some camps give city kids, who might otherwise spend their vacations inside
20 watching TV, a chance to explore country life. Some camps send special invitations to kids with health problems, such as diabetes or cancer. There are also camps for children with physical disabilities. And still others that serve children from families where a parent was disabled in a war. What these camps all have in common is that they offer kids an opportunity to **bond** with others while learning sports, art, music,
25 or school subjects in a natural environment.

Fresh Air

Since 1877, nearly two million kids from New York City have taken summer vacations thanks to the Fresh Air Fund. Some go to traditional camps, where canoeing, swimming, campfires, and art are part of the everyday activities. At these camps, children live in cabins or tents and sleep in bunks .

The Fresh Air Fund also sponsors less **conventional** types of vacations. Thousands of children go to the homes of carefully selected host families in various suburban or rural communities in one of 13 northeast states in the United States or in Canada.

Together, the host family and the child decide how the child will spend his or her time. Children may go bike riding in the country roads. They may choose to fish, swim, play soccer, or see a parade. After all it's their vacation.

Many host families have children of their own. In that case, the kids do what kids do—hang out, play ball, or get ice cream, always accompanied by the adults.

"I cried on the bus going there," said one 10-year-old boy, "because I was scared." But the host family had two sons of their own and the three boys got along great. "We ate spaghetti. I touched a worm in the yard. Their house is the best."

"When I was seven, I stayed with a family upstate for a week," says one 38-year-old woman. "I still remember going biking and catching a salamander. Best of all, after all these years I'm still friends with the girl I met there. I love that family."

1. How are some Fresh Air vacations different from traditional summer camps?

_____

2. Where do many Fresh Air kids live during the rest of the year?

_____

Continue reading to find out about other types of camps. Ask yourself questions.

Attention!

Some summer programs are exclusively for kids with parents in the U.S. military. Operation Purple, for example, operates at 34 locations in 26 states.

The Lazy W Ranch in San Juan Capistrano, California, is for children of military men or women wounded after 9/11. Kids from nine to 14 can go swimming, horseback riding, and play basketball and volleyball. There are special events, too, such as a Hawaiian **luau,** and a western night, when kids play cowboys and cowgirls.

Children at Operation Purple often feel a special bond with other campers. They all know the difficulties the family faces when a parent has been hurt in a war. So camp is a time to heal emotionally. Said Andrea, a 13-year-old, "I still worry about my dad when I'm away. Sure, I can swim or shoot hoops, but it makes me feel better when I write home." Added the girl's mom, "Andrea sent 13 postcards. They cheered up my husband. Every child should have a chance to go to camp."

Hole in the Wall

Why shouldn't children with cancer or diabetes go to camp? Just like all kids, kids with illnesses respond well to the unique quality of the camp experience. They **relish** the warm, **supportive** camping atmosphere in the great outdoors.

One such camp is Hole in the Wall, which hosts more than 1,000 children between the ages of 7 and 15. With nurses and doctors on staff to meet the children's medical needs, the counselors involve the kids in canoe trips, theater,

65 tennis, arts and crafts, as well as hot air balloon trips. What's more, the kids also visit an animal farm or play baseball. What child wouldn't want to go there?

Planned activities aside, sometimes kids simply need comfort and encouragement to face another injection or another day, so fellow campers and counselors support each other, telling jokes, sharing stories, or singing camp songs.

70 Sadly, some kids are just too ill to go to camp. In those cases, Camp Hole in the Wall in New England becomes Camp-in-a-Suitcase. Whether the campers are in the hospital, in a clinic, or at home, the counselors from Camp-in-a-Suitcase create the flavor of camp, raising the spirits of some very sick children.

3. Why would a young boy cry on the bus on his way to summer camp?

_____

4. A fact can be proven true. An opinion is a personal belief. Is the statement that Hole in the Wall hosts more than 1,000 kids a fact or an opinion? Explain.

_____

Finish reading to find out what some parents think about summer camp.

Where's Your Bunk?

75 There are also camps for learning-disabled children. No matter what the disability, children participate in traditional camp activities like boating and swimming. Counselors and medical staff are there to help them do it safely.

Sometimes children at camps for the learning disabled participate in regular camp activities in the morning and school instruction in the afternoon. Some camps combine
80 the two by assigning the campers projects, such as creating the camp newsletter with photos and articles about the counselors, the campers, and camp life in general.

One 11-year-old explained it this way, "I brought my summer reading and the counselors helped me understand the books. There were no tests, but I learned a lot."

More Benefits

85 The rewards of camp life can be enormous. Said one mother of a physically-disabled child, "Before Donna got on the camp bus, she didn't talk. When she got home, she could point to things outside her window and say the word. This was a huge step. Donna's counselors were great with her."

Other parents also notice a difference in their kids after camp. Said one father,
90 "Mike is an overactive, sometimes violent kid. But after two weeks at camp, he was calmer. He didn't fly off the handle as much." He added, "For the first time in a long time, Mike was proud of himself. Camp was a positive experience for him."

Reported one grandmother, "Teisha used to slouch a lot. She didn't care how she looked. When she got back from camp, she was still the same kid. Only more
95 confident. Friendlier with people. Camp was wonderful."

There's no doubt about it. Camp has the potential to promote the physical, social, emotional, and academic lives of children, indoors, outdoors, and with new friends.

Volleyball, anyone?

5. What kinds of social or emotional changes can kids make at camp?

_____

physically disabled (noun)
handicapped, crippled, or injured; deprived of specific physical abilities

slouch (verb)
to sit or walk in a lazy or tired way, with shoulders and head down

After You Read

Build a robust vocabulary.

Writing Sentences   Write a complete sentence to respond to each of the following questions or statements. Use the underlined word in your answer. Use the definitions on page 45 to help you.

1.   What does your morning <u>routine</u> include?

_____

2.   What do people often do or wear at a <u>luau</u>?

_____

3.   Name something you <u>relish</u> doing on the weekends.

_____

4.   What is one <u>environmental</u> problem we have today?

_____

5.   Describe a time when someone was <u>supportive</u> of you.

_____

Sentence Completions   Complete each sentence using a word from the box.

acquire	bond	cater	conventional	environment
exclusively	luau	relish	routine	supportive

1.   That camp is _____ for girls.

2.   It's _____ to dress baby girls in pink and baby boys in blue.

3.   Glenn hoped to _____ new skills at computer camp.

4.   Some camps _____ to kids who enjoy riding horses.

5.   Doing a project together is an excellent way for campers to _____ with each other.

Word Building Suffixes   A **suffix** is a group of letters added to the end of a word. When a suffix is added, a new word with a new meaning is formed. Look at the chart below. It shows some common suffixes and their meanings.

Suffix	Meaning
–al	relating to
–ful	full of
–ness	the state or quality of being
-ly	in a certain manner

Read these words. Each word ends with a suffix. Draw a circle around the suffix in each word.

fully	happily	thoughtful	kindness	original

Use the meaning of the suffix to help you figure out what the word means. Then use each word in a sentence.

1. fully: _____

2. happily: _____

3. thoughtful: _____

4. kindness: _____

5. original: _____

TIP: When you read, you may notice words with suffixes. If you remember what the suffix means, you may be able to figure out the meaning of a new word.

Writing Activity   Write a short paragraph that correctly uses key vocabulary words to tell about a vacation you once took. Use at least four of the words from the list on page 45. Reread the definitions, if necessary.

_____

_____

_____

_____

_____

Think about your reading.

Check your comprehension.   Answer each question. If you don't know the answer, reread the lines in parentheses.

1. What do most summer camps have in common? (lines 23–25)

_____

2. What makes Operation Purple unique? (lines 46–47)

_____

3. What might Hole in the Wall camp do if a sick child can't leave the hospital? (lines 70–73)

_____

4. What are some benefits of going to camp? (lines 96–97)

_____

Use reading skills: Distinguish fact and opinion.

A **fact** is a statement that is true. A fact, such as "The couch is six feet long," can be checked or confirmed. An **opinion** is a personal belief or judgment, such as "Vanilla ice cream is better than strawberry ice cream." It may be supported by fact, but it cannot be proved.

Distinguish fact and opinion. As you read "What Happens at Summer Camp?" you came across some facts and opinions about camp. Reread the following paragraph.

> "Andrea sent 13 postcards. They cheered up my husband. Every child should have a chance to go to camp."

1. Find a sentence that states a fact. Underline it.

2. Find a sentence that states an opinion. Circle it.

Use a graphic organizer.

The article contains many facts and opinions. Here are one fact and one opinion from the article. In the table below, add other facts and opinions.

Facts	Opinions
1. Andrea sent 13 postcards.	Every child should have a chance to go to camp.
2.	
3.	
4.	

Write about it.

Write a description.

Imagine that your sister is thinking of sending her disabled six-year-old son to summer camp for two weeks. She heard that you know a lot about camps. She asks your opinion about sending Max to a camp 200 miles away for two weeks.

Write a description of what camp is like. Talk about the activities and the counselors. Explain the benefits of camp life and also describe any negatives. Give your opinion about whether your sister should send Max to camp.

Prewriting   On your own or with a partner, fill in the chart with facts and your opinions about summer camp.

Facts	Opinions
Max will meet other kids just like him.	It'll be good for him to be away from home.

Thinking Beyond Reading Think about these questions and discuss them with a partner. Add ideas to the graphic organizer as you talk.

- What kinds of activities are at summer camp?

- Who do children meet at camp?

- How do children grow physically, emotionally, and socially at camp?

- What are some other benefits of camping?

Write a draft. Write a first draft of your description. Your description might begin with this topic sentence: "I know that you are thinking of sending Max to camp." Provide some facts about what campers typically do at camp. Add information that tells who would be there to make sure Max has a safe and fun experience. Give your opinion of whether Max should go to camp.

Use the ideas in your chart to help you write your description. Add as many details as you can.

_____

_____

_____

_____

_____

_____

_____

_____

_____

_____

_____

_____

_____

Revise and create a final draft. Write your final draft on a separate piece of paper. As you revise, check your draft for these specific points.

- Did you include facts to support your position why Max should or shouldn't go to camp?

- Did you support your opinions with facts?

- Did you check spelling and grammar to make sure your writing is clear and correct?

Help in an Emergency

Learning Objectives

In this lesson you will:

- Read a story about firefighters and others who arrive first at a disaster scene.

- Identify cause and effect.

- Master the key vocabulary used in the story.

- Write a summary of the story.

Key Vocabulary

commotion *(noun)* confusion; noisy rushing about

dilemma *(noun)* a difficult choice

disoriented *(adjective)* confused about where you are

engulfed *(verb)* swallowed up or flooded

grimaced *(verb)* made a facial expression of disapproval or pain

maelstrom *(noun)* a state in which things are very confused and upset

maneuvering *(verb)* moving skillfully

potentially *(adverb)* possibly

spewing *(verb)* pouring out

tersely *(adverb)* using only a few words

Before You Read

As you read this story, get involved from the beginning. Predict what you think the story will be about. Then, as you read, keep making predictions about what you think will happen next. Also, visualize, or form pictures in your mind, about what you are reading, These active reading strategies will help you understand and enjoy the story.

Make predictions.

1. What do the title and the illustration tell you the story will be about?

   I think the story will be about a fire.

   _____

   _____

   _____

   _____

2. Who do you think the characters in the story will be?

   _____

   _____

   _____

   _____

3. What do you think might happen in the story?

   _____

   _____

   _____

   _____

Visualize while you read.

1. Read the second paragraph of the story. What picture do you get in your mind from the description of the fire?

   This must be a big fire with flames, smoke, and an explosion. I think a lot of people were hurt.

   _____

   _____

   _____

   _____

Burning

Make a prediction. Will James Pasquini's courage be wasted in the deadly fumes of a chemical fire? Read to find out. Then put a star in the margin when you know the answer to the question.

The gigantic boom rocked James Pasquini and the ten other firefighters at the firehouse.

"Whoa!" Pasquini yelled, feeling a bit **disoriented** from the huge blast. Seconds later the siren at the firehouse began wailing. The report came over
5 the radio: It was an explosion in a chemical plant and workers were missing. Flames were higher than the sides of the factory, and tanks of **potentially** explosive chemicals were dangerously close to the raging fire. A gigantic funnel of black smoke was billowing from the site, **spewing** toxic substances into the air. The hazmat team was on the way, its specialists outfitted with masks and
10 protective gear to keep out the toxic chemicals.

"This is a bad one," Pasquini thought.

Things were worse by the time Pasquini and the other first responders got to the scene. The black, oily smoke was so thick it darkened the sky. This was no ordinary smoke; it made the firefighters gasp. Pasquini took a lungful and
15 felt sick to his stomach, with an instant headache.

By the time Pasquini and the other firefighters got there, all but two of the workers had been accounted for. Other workers ran in circles in blind panic. A few burned people moaned as medical workers lifted them onto gurneys and into ambulances. Hard hats from the factory workers who had heard the
20 explosion and run littered the blacktop outside the plant, and huge pieces of broken concrete and plates of twisted metal made **maneuvering** difficult for

toxic *(adjective)*
capable of causing illness or death

hazmat *(adjective)*
hazardous or dangerous materials

first responders *(noun)*
the first workers to get to a disaster scene, such as police officers, firefighters, and medical workers

gurneys *(noun)*
stretchers or cots on wheels

the firefighters. The hazmat truck hadn't arrived yet. It had to come from a distant fire station.

1. Why does Pasquini think, "This is a bad one"?

_____

_____

Until the hazmat team arrives, the firefighters are on their own in the dangerous fire. Underline what they try to do to stay safe while they fight the fire.

The captain of Pasquini's station gathered the firefighters. "Listen up," he
25 said **tersely.** "We don't have much. We don't have information on what the
heck is burning, and how toxic it is. We don't have anything on what's in the
tanks or where the tanks are. We know it's a dye manufacturer. That's bad.
Some of the stuff that makes up dyes is wicked. For now, I'm most worried
about that hissing. To me, it says tanks about to blow. All we can try to do is
30 stay as far away as we can and still try to direct some water on those tanks to
cool them off, keep them from blowing." He shook his head. "Bad."
"Aren't there two people in there somewhere?" asked Pasquini's buddy,
Tel Guffey. The captain rubbed his chin and **grimaced.**
"Yeah," he admitted. "Somewhere. But we got no idea where." He gestured at
35 the roaring black smoke that **engulfed** the building. "Where do you even start?"
Pasquini and his team followed orders, pulling the hose close enough to
reach the hissing tanks. "Stay away from the actual fires in the tanks," the
captain shouted above the roar. "We don't know if the water will make the fire
worse or better."
40 Nearby, Pasquini could see a guy in a shirt and tie frantically looking with
the chief through sheets of paper in a file. "I don't know if these are the right
diagrams that tell what's where," he was yelling. "Joe and Tom, they'd know
better, but both of them got burned. They're in ambulances headed for the
hospital. This was all I could find."

2. Why is the captain worried about the hissing tanks?

_____

_____

3. Why are the factory workers having trouble finding the right plans for the plant?

_____

_____

At a fire like this, firefighters have to make split-second, often dangerous decisions. Put an arrow in the margin when you learn what decision Pasquini makes at the fire.

45   Meanwhile, Pasquini and the others could tell this was no normal smoke. They choked in the fumes, wondering what they were breathing and wondering if they should retreat until they learned more. As Pasquini gasped, there was a break in the fierce crackle of the fire. In that moment, Pasquini heard a moan.

50   Now he had a real **dilemma.** Pretend he heard nothing and keep himself safe, or go in, risking his own life. He could kill himself trying to be a hero and still do nothing to save whoever was moaning.

It didn't take long for Pasquini to make up his mind. He gave his place on the hose to another firefighter, held his breath, and plunged into the

55   **maelstrom.** Inside, he stayed as low as he could, below the bitter black smoke, and saw the two missing workers. One was burned on the back and arms. The other was crumpled, perhaps blown into a steel beam when the explosion hit. He was face up, bleeding from his mouth. The moans were coming from him. Pasquini scooped him up, holding his breath in the stinging smoke and wincing at the extreme heat. He carried the bleeding man out, laid him

60   down on the concrete, and immediately went back in. In another 30 seconds, Pasquini carried out the burned worker, a woman, on his back.

There was an uproar and more **commotion** as Pasquini brought out the second worker. An ambulance was already wailing away with the first worker,

65   a man. A second ambulance was waiting for the other victim.

The ambulances radioed back, knowing Pasquini would want to know. The woman was dead, burned over too much of her body to survive. The man, though, would live. Pasquini hid a smile of triumph as his buddies slapped him on the back. "Whatever," he shrugged. "That's what we do, eh?"

4. What does Pasquini hear during a break in the fire's roar?

    _____

    _____

5. What happens to the two people Pasquini brings out?

    _____

    _____

After You Read

Build a robust vocabulary.

Writing Sentences   Write a complete sentence to respond to each of the following questions or statements. Use the underlined word in your answer. Use the definitions on page 55 to help you.

1. Tell about a <u>dilemma</u> you once faced.

    _____

2. Where might you see smoke <u>spewing</u> into the sky?

    _____

3. Tell about a time when you <u>grimaced</u>.

    _____

4. Why might you speak to someone <u>tersely</u>?

    _____

5. What can cause a <u>commotion</u>?

    _____

Sentence Completions   Complete each sentence using a word from the box.

commotion	dilemma	disoriented	engulfed	grimaced
maelstrom	maneuvering	potentially	spewing	tersely

1. I woke up _____ and wasn't sure where I was.

2. When flames _____ the building, we couldn't see its outlines.

3. That new way of fighting fires may _____ be best, but so far it doesn't work better than the way we have now.

4. He found _____ through the tight spaces difficult.

5. The _____ was frightening to those of us caught in it.

Word Building   Look at the following words. What is the same about them all?

kickboard	lawbreaker	sandblast	inland

Each word is made up of two smaller words. They are **compound words.** Draw a line between the two parts of each word. Compare your answers with a partner's. Discuss what each word means, using the meaning of each part of the word to help you define it.

Write the meaning of each of these compound words. Then use each word in a sentence.

1. firefighter: _____

_____

2. firebomb: _____

_____

3. firewood: _____

_____

4. firewall: _____

_____

5. firestorm: _____

_____

TIP: If you see a long word you do not know, check to see if it is a compound word. Try to take apart the word, look at the smaller words, and then figure out the compound word.

Writing Activity   Write a short paragraph that correctly uses key vocabulary words to tell what happened in the fire from James Pasquini's point of view. Use at least four of the words from the list on page 55. Reread the definitions, if necessary.

_____

_____

_____

Think about your reading.

Check your comprehension.   Answer each question. If you don't know the answer, reread the lines in parentheses.

1. Why does it take a long time for the hazmat truck to reach the fire? (lines 22–23)

_____

2. Why does the captain tell the firefighters not to put water on the fires in the tanks? (lines 37–39)

_____

3. What dilemma does Pasquini face when he hears the moans in the fire? (lines 50–52)

_____

4. What does Pasquini say about why he rescued the two workers? (lines 68–69)

_____

Use reading skills: Identify cause and effect.

Identifying **causes** and **effects** helps you better understand what you read. You see why things happen (the causes) and what happens as a result (the effects). In this story, many of the events before and during the fire are either causes or effects. Sometimes an effect can become the cause of a later event.

Identify cause and effect. Read this section of the story and look for causes and effects.

> A few burned people moaned as medical workers lifted them onto gurneys and into ambulances. Hard hats from the factory workers who had heard the explosion and run littered the blacktop outside the plant, and huge pieces of broken concrete and plates of twisted metal made maneuvering difficult for the firefighters.

1. What happened (the effect) when the burned people were lifted onto the gurneys?

   _____

2. What caused hard hats to litter the blacktop?

   _____

Use a graphic organizer.

You can use a graphic organizer like the one below to help you decide what are causes and what are effects. Fill in the boxes to help you think about events in the story.

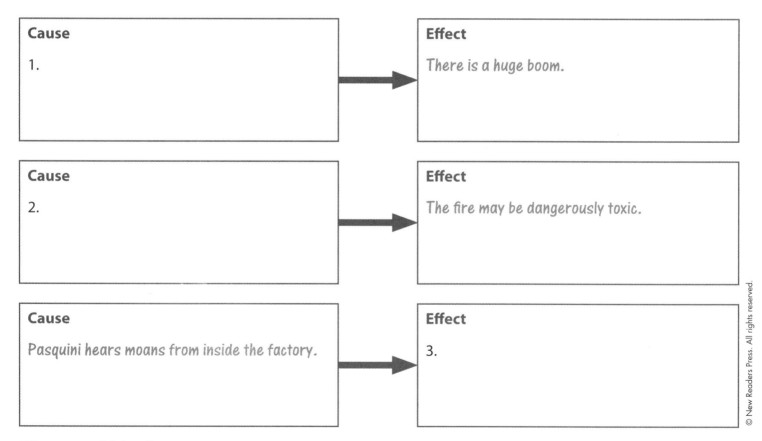

Cause	Effect
1.	There is a huge boom.
2.	The fire may be dangerously toxic.
Pasquini hears moans from inside the factory.	3.

Write about it.

Write a summary.

Write a summary of this story. When you read your summary, you should feel that it tells the most important points of the story. Someone who is reading the summary should understand the beginning, middle, and end of the story.

Prewriting   A graphic organizer in which you write phrases that tell the most important things that happen in the beginning, middle, and end of the story can help you organize information for your summary. The Beginning is already done for you. Complete the boxes for Middle and End. Include as many points as you need in each box.

Beginning

- Gigantic boom
- Pasquini and other firefighters head for chemical plant fire

↓

Middle

↓

End

Thinking Beyond Reading   Think about these questions and discuss them with a partner. Add ideas to the graphic organizer as you talk.

- What qualities and skills does it take to make a good firefighter?

- Did the firefighters show enough caution, or too much, before the hazmat truck got there?

- Did Pasquini make a good choice in going in to find the two workers inside the plant?

Write a draft.   Write a first draft of your summary. Use the graphic organizer to help you. Your summary might begin like this: "After Pasquini hears a gigantic boom and a siren, he and the other firefighters rush to a huge fire in a chemical plant."

_____

_____

_____

_____

_____

_____

_____

_____

_____

_____

_____

_____

_____

_____

_____

_____

_____

_____

Revise and create a final draft.   Write your final draft on a separate piece of paper. As you revise, check your draft for these specific points.

- Did you include all the important events that happened in the story?

- Does the summary organize events from beginning to middle to end?

- Did you check spelling and grammar to make sure your writing is clear and correct?

A Sports Icon

Learning Objectives

In this lesson you will:

▨ Learn about golfer Tiger Woods.

▨ Recognize time order.

▨ Master the key vocabulary used in the article.

▨ Write about the people and events that influenced a person's life.

Key Vocabulary

composure *(noun)* calmness

discipline *(noun)* the ability to control your own behavior

dominated *(verb)* was the most successful and influential

integrity *(noun)* the quality of being honest and having high moral standards

mentor *(verb)* to advise and help less experienced and knowledgeable people

prestigious *(adjective)* respected

promising *(adjective)* likely to be successful in the future

stamina *(noun)* physical or mental strength that lets you do something for a long time without getting tired

surpassing *(verb)* doing something better than someone else

witnessed *(verb)* saw something happen

Before You Read

Using what you know is a good active reading strategy that some readers use to help them understand and remember what they read. Active readers also summarize the important ideas in an article as they read. They write down their summaries or summarize in their heads.

Use what you know.

1. What's your favorite sport?

   _____

   _____

   _____

   _____

2. Who's your favorite professional player?

   _____

   _____

   _____

   _____

3. Why do you like this sport or player?

   _____

   _____

   _____

   _____

THINK ABOUT IT

My all-time favorite player is basketball star Michael Jordan. I liked how he used to fly through the air. I miss seeing his energy on the court. I wish he hadn't retired.

Summarize.

1. After you read a section of the story, try summarizing what happened in that section. In a few of your own words, write down what happened.

   _____

   _____

   _____

   _____

Who Is Tiger Woods?

Read the following article to learn about Tiger Woods's life and career. Write notes in the margin summarizing important things that happened in his life.

Do you have a favorite sports figure you love to watch on TV or whom you adored as a kid? Was it football star Walter Payton? How about soccer champion Mia Hamm? Or boxing great Oscar de la Hoya? What about the legendary Muhammad Ali?

5 Many people from all around the world might choose professional golfer, Tiger Woods. Tiger Woods is a remarkable athlete who has **dominated** his sport since he was just a boy.

Early Years

Tiger Woods was born in 1975 in a city outside of Los Angeles. His father, 10 Earl, was part African American and part Native American. His mother, Kultida, is part Chinese, part Thai, and part white. Earl and Kultida named their baby Eldrick. But Earl, a former army lieutenant , nicknamed him Tiger, to honor Earl's Vietnamese pal, whom he met in the army. Earl explained, "I called my son Tiger, hoping he'd grow up to be as courageous as my friend."

15 Tiger Woods showed an interest in golf even as a baby. Playing in his crib, the boy imitated his father as he hit golf balls. And in 1977, at the age of two, Tiger's golf swing was so strong that he showed it off on TV.

A few years after his TV appearance, *Golf Digest* wrote an article about the rising star. Sports writers and reporters starting calling Tiger a golf prodigy . 20 The rest of the world waited and watched to see how far this **promising** young man would go. It wasn't long before they **witnessed** the development of an amazing athlete.

lieutenant *(noun)*
a rank for a junior officer in the military

prodigy *(noun)*
a child who has a great natural ability in a skill

1. Why did Earl Woods nickname his son Tiger?

_____

2. When did news reporters and writers label Tiger a golf prodigy?

_____

Continue reading to find out how Tiger succeeded as a teenager. As you read, make summarizing notes in the margin of the major events that occurred as Tiger went through high school.

Competitiveness Emerges

25 With his gift and a desire to succeed, Tiger started to enter golf tournaments. In 1983, when he was eight, he won his first international junior golf competition. But Tiger wanted more, so he practiced and learned the finer points of the game. The next year, at age nine, he was an even better golfer. He won the same competition, and then again, when he was 12, 13, 14, and 15 years old.

30 Tiger's Dedication

At around this time, Tiger decided that he wanted to be a world-class golfer and that to do so, he needed to devote himself to the sport. First he made sure he was physically fit. He trained for hours every day. He worked out, improving his strength and **stamina.** He ate right. And he practiced all the physical and 35 mental aspects of golf. Tiger excelled at every step. Perhaps his only weakness was his eyesight. He would later have surgery to correct his vision.

Tiger's parents made sure that he was well educated. After high school, Tiger attended the **prestigious** Stanford University in California. Said his father, "The only thing better than a good person is an educated person."

40 Family Influence

No one doubts that Tiger's family has played a big role in his success. His mother taught him **discipline,** something all professionals need to succeed. His father taught him golf form and technique. His father also taught him something else that was nearly as valuable—concentration. As Tiger practiced, 45 Earl deliberately made noise from the sidelines, trying to distract him. Said his dad years later, "I was using golf to teach him about life. How to handle responsibility and pressure." Earl's strategy worked, as Tiger is known today for his **composure** on the course. The values and strong work ethic that Tiger learned as a kid contributed to his success as an adult.

50 By the age of 20, Tiger had won so many amateur tournaments that the sports world predicted again that he would one day grow up to dominate the golf world. They were correct. Right before he turned pro, Tiger received a great honor. In 1996 _Sports Illustrated_ named him Sportsman of the Year, **surpassing** many talented and more experienced players from other sports. And at age 21, 55 he won the Masters, one of the world's most important golf tournaments.

amateur _(adjective)_
for enjoyment, but
not for money

This was big news. Tiger Woods was the youngest player ever to win the Masters. And he was the first person of color and of Asian background to do so.

3. What was Tiger's one physical weakness? What did he do about it?

_____

4. Why was 1996 a special year for Tiger Woods?

_____

Finish reading the article to learn what else Tiger Woods achieved in golf as he got older.

What is the secret to his success? Woods says a lot of it has to do with being flexible. After winning his first Masters, he said, "Every day on the golf course is
60 about making little adjustments, taking what you've got on that day and finding the way to deal with it." He also says that the values his parents and his other teachers taught him—**integrity,** honesty, discipline, and responsibility—keep him focused and strong.

Pushes On
65 In his early 20s, Woods was almost unstoppable on the golf course. In 1996, he made history by winning all four major golf titles: the U.S. Masters, the U.S. Open, the British Open, and the Professional Golf Association (PGA) Championship, each with a large monetary prize. Today he's a wealthy man, making millions by winning more tournaments and by endorsing athletic products.
70 Woods stands out for other reasons as well. While other athletes may not always behave well, Woods has a reputation as a gentleman, on and off the course. He also has a great sense of humor.
Given Woods's values, it is not surprising that he chooses to **mentor** children. In 1996, he and his father established the Tiger Woods Foundation.
75 The foundation helps millions of kids reach their dreams. It awards scholarships and grants and sets up junior golf teams to help children succeed in the sport and in life.
Still a relatively young man in his 30s, Woods has already made a major contribution to the game of golf and to lifting the spirits of kids. With so many
80 years ahead of him, it is clear that Tiger Woods will make an impact on the world for decades to come.

endorsing (verb)
saying that you approve of someone or something

5. How did Tiger make history in 1996?

_____

6. How does Tiger Woods help children?

_____

After You Read

Build a robust vocabulary.

Writing Sentences   Write a complete sentence to respond to each of the following questions or statements. Use the underlined word in your answer. Use the definitions on page 65 to help you.

1. Tell about a time when you lost your <u>composure</u>.

   _____

2. Which famous person would you choose to <u>mentor</u> you?

   _____

3. What do you do that requires <u>discipline</u>?

   _____

4. Name an athlete other than Tiger Woods who <u>dominated</u> his or her game.

   _____

5. Explain how someone who cheats on a test lacks <u>integrity</u>.

   _____

Sentence Completions   Complete each sentence using a word from the box.

composure	discipline	dominated	integrity	mentor
prestigious	promising	stamina	surpassing	witnessed

1. Debra's music teacher told her that she had a _____ career as a drummer.

2. When you can play ball for a long time, you show you have a lot of _____.

3. We _____ a car accident on our way to school.

4. Name a _____ tournament that Tiger Woods has won.

5. Each time Bob runs, he gets faster and faster, always _____ his earlier speed.

Word Building   If you want to compare two things, you usually add *-er* to the root word, for example, the *longer* table, the *shorter* table, or the *taller* table. With words that end in *y*, you change the *y* to *i* when you add *-er*. For example, *happy* becomes *happier* and *easy* becomes *easier*.

Read these words. Circle the ending that shows that the word is comparing two things.

rounder	fatter	wider	happier

Add an ending to each word below so that it is a word that compares. Use each of the words in a sentence that compares two things.

1. cold: _____

_____

2. funny: _____

_____

3. light: _____

_____

4. heavy: _____

_____

5. hot: _____

_____

Writing Activity   Write a short paragraph that correctly uses key vocabulary words to tell about an athlete or sports team that you know a lot about. Use at least four of the words from the list on page 65. Reread the definitions, if necessary.

_____

_____

_____

_____

Think about your reading.

Check your comprehension.   Answer each question. If you don't know the answer, reread the lines in parentheses.

1. What are two ways Tiger showed his talent for golf before the age of three? (lines 15–17)

_____

2. What did Tiger do as a teenager to improve his chances of becoming a world-class player? (lines 31–35)

_____

3. When Earl Woods made distracting noises, what did that teach Tiger about playing golf? (lines 43–49)

_____

4. Why was winning the Masters the first time a big event for Tiger? (lines 56–57)

_____

Use reading skills: Recognize time order.

When you read about a person, the passage is often organized in chronological order, the order in which the events took place in that person's life. If you understand **time order,** you can better understand what's going on. An author may show time order by using words such as *first, then, next,* or *last.* Or, she may give dates or ages to show when things happened. As you read, watch for words or dates that indicate when an event occurred.

Recognize time order.   The author of "Who Is Tiger Woods?" organized the article from Tiger's birth to the present day—that is, in the order that things happened. Reread the following paragraph from the section called "Competitiveness Emerges."

> With his gift and a desire to succeed, Tiger started to enter golf tournaments. In 1983, when he was eight, he won his first international junior golf competition. But Tiger wanted more, so he practiced and learned the finer points of the game. The next year, at age nine, he was an even better golfer. He won the same competition, and then again, when he was 12, 13, 14, and 15 years old.

1.   What did Tiger do when he was eight years old?

   _____

2.   What did he do the following year?

   _____

3.   At what ages did Tiger win again?

   _____

Use a graphic organizer.

You can use a time line like the one below to show events in time order. Write the letter of each event where it belongs on the time line below.

a.   Was taught to ignore noisy distractions.

b.   Was named to honor a friend of his father's.

c.   Learned to be flexible.

d.   Showed his integrity by teaching kids and awarding them scholarships.

e.   Was encouraged to make education a priority in his life.

Birth (1975)	**School** (to teens)	**College** (teens to 20s)	**Masters Champ** (age 21)	**Adult**
_____	_____	_____	_____	_____

Write about it.

Write about the people and events that influenced a person's life.

On your own or with a partner brainstorm a list of people who you respect for their character and values. Think about friends, family members, people in your community, or people in the news. You will write a paragraph that explains how one person from your list developed the qualities that people respect in him or her.

Prewriting   On your own or with a partner, choose one of the people from your list. Think about how the different people in his or her life helped that person develop. Make a time line to show events in time order. Use as many lines as you need.

Date	Event

Thinking Beyond Reading   Think about these questions and discuss them with a partner. Add ideas to your time line as you talk.

- Who were the most important people in this person's life?

- What qualities does this person have that you respect?

- How did he or she develop those qualities?

Write a draft.   Write a first draft that identifies important events in the person's life and shows how people and events influenced who he or she has become as a person. Use the time line that you developed to organize your thoughts. Think about the order of events as you write. Be as detailed as you can be.

_____

_____

_____

_____

_____

_____

_____

_____

_____

_____

_____

_____

_____

_____

_____

_____

Revise and create a final draft.   Write your final draft on a separate piece of paper. As you revise, check your draft for these specific points.

- Did you include the most important events and influences in the person's life?

- Did you check spelling and grammar to make sure your writing is clear and correct?

Flying High

Learning Objectives

In this lesson, you will:

▩ Learn about Amelia Earhart's contributions to aviation.

▩ Draw conclusions from the article.

▩ Master the key vocabulary used in the article.

▩ Write a letter to the editor.

Key Vocabulary

advocate *(noun)* someone who speaks in favor of a cause

aviation *(noun)* the field of aircraft manufacture and operation

determination *(noun)* the quality of continuing to work at something even when it is difficult

distinguished *(adjective)* marked by excellence

evidence *(noun)* proof of something

foretell *(verb)* predict

independence *(noun)* the quality of not relying on others

innovator *(noun)* a person who does something in a new way

raging *(verb)* being out of control

trailblazer *(noun)* a pioneer in a particular field

Before You Read

The article you are about to read is about Amelia Earhart, a famous woman from long ago who flew airplanes. As an active reader, ask yourself what you already know about her or about flying. Keep asking yourself questions about what you read in the article and look for the answers.

Use what you know.

1. What do you know about Amelia Earhart or about the history of flying?

   _____

   _____

   _____

I think I've seen Amelia Earhart's name, maybe in a history book. Maybe there was even a movie about her.

2. Have you or has someone you know ever traveled on a plane? What was the destination?

   _____

   _____

   _____

3. Would you like to pilot a plane? Why or why not?

   _____

   _____

   _____

Ask yourself questions.

1. Why were articles and books written about Amelia Earhart? (Read the first two paragraphs of the article.)

   _____

   _____

   _____

When did Amelia Earhart live? What exactly did she do? The title says she disappeared. What's that about?

2. Was Earhart interested in planes and flying even when she was a kid? (Read the third paragraph.)

   _____

   _____

   _____

The Disappearance of Amelia Earhart

Read the following article to find out about Amelia Earhart's life. Jot down in the margins questions you have as you read.

Have you checked the newspaper headlines today? What did you find? A surprising discovery of a dinosaur fossil? A fire **raging** out of control in the West? A major sports upset?

In 1928 newspapers were filled with stories about Amelia Earhart, the first woman
5 to fly across the Atlantic Ocean. But 1928 wasn't the only year in which Earhart would make news, as papers throughout the 1930s were filled with other stories about her successes in the air. In fact, to this day, Earhart is remembered in books and articles as one of the greatest pilots of the 20th century and as a woman of spirit and bravery.

Indifference, At First

10 Amelia Earhart was born in 1897 to a wealthy family in Kansas. As a child, she showed little interest in planes or flying. In fact, when she was 10 years old, she saw her first plane and described it as "a thing of rusty wire and wood." The plane did not hold her attention.

But Earhart did show an interest in unusual careers for women. In her
15 bedroom, she kept an album of news clippings about women who had succeeded in careers that were at the time reserved for men. These careers included law, film directing, and engineering. Her interest in these fields would **foretell** her eventual role as a leader in a nontraditional field for women, **aviation.**

When did Amelia's interest in aviation emerge? She was 23. A pilot offered
20 her a ride on his plane, handing her a helmet and goggles . She boarded and the plane took off. When it reached 300 feet, Amelia felt gleeful as she soared in the air. At that moment she decided she had to fly.

How could she afford it? At first, Earhart had to earn money for flying lessons. She got a job as a nurse's aide and later as a social worker. She saved her earnings

helmet *(noun)*
  a hard hat to protect the head during sports or dangerous activities

goggles *(noun)*
  special glasses to protect the eyes

25 and was able to afford flying lessons the following year, receiving instruction from a female pilot. Six months later she bought her first plane.

1. What did Amelia do as a child that showed she might one day have an unusual career?

   _____

2. At what age did Amelia become interested in flying?

   _____

Continue reading the article to find out how Earhart made a name for herself in aviation. Ask yourself questions as you read and look for answers.

Gaining Recognition

It didn't take long for Earhart to get recognition for flying. In 1922 she broke a record for female pilots by reaching 14,000 feet, the first woman to fly at that height.
30 The news media eagerly reported on it. She broke other records as well, and before long the Boston Globe called her "one of the best women pilots in the United States." She also joined the National Aeronautics Association, an organization dominated by men. She firmly believed that female pilots were as skilled as male pilots.

One day Earhart received a phone call that would change her life. "How
35 would you like to be the first woman to fly across the Atlantic?" the man who would later become her husband asked. Although the position was as a passenger, not as a pilot, Earhart accepted the offer and was given the job of keeping the plane's log, while two men piloted.

Back then, even car travel was rare, so when a woman flew across the Atlantic,
40 newspapers took note. Earhart flew on the plane, and when it landed, reporters flocked around "the girl." In fact, it was Earhart's photograph that appeared on the front pages of newspapers worldwide.

Earhart was eager to prove that women could succeed in aviation. She continued taking flying lessons, learning how to read the instruments and
45 developing the coordination and concentration needed to pilot a plane. A few years later, Earhart made history once more. In 1932, Earhart crossed the Atlantic by plane again, but this time, she was the pilot on the nonstop trip, not a passenger.

The trip was noteworthy indeed. But the way she flew made it unique as well. Since she flew solo, she had to find a way to stay awake throughout the long trip.
50 Very much an **innovator,** Earhart kept herself awake with smelling salts, not coffee, as other pilots would have done. What about her meals? She ate lightly, sipping soup from a thermos bottle and tomato juice from a can.

By the time Earhart landed safely, her reputation as an aviator was established. She went on to give lectures and write articles. She granted interviews. And of
55 course, she flew planes, breaking more records.

Were Earhart's accomplishments recognized in other ways? Yes. She was the first woman to receive the **Distinguished** Flying Cross award from Congress. In addition, then-president Herbert Hoover presented her with a gold medal from the National Geographic Society. Both were important awards.

log (noun)
   a daily record

smelling salts (noun)
   a preparation of ammonium carbonate and ammonia water used as a stimulant

3. How did Earhart improve her flying skills?

_____

4. What awards did Earhart receive?

_____

Finish reading to find out what happened to Earhart.

Beginning of the End

60   By 1937 Amelia Earhart was a household name, known for her flying abilities, her **independence,** and her **determination.** She added to that fame by writing a number of best-selling books. She was also an **advocate** for women's rights, helping to form The Ninety-Nines, a women's pilot organization.

65   While Earhart loved challenges, her last adventure would lead to tragedy. On June 1, 1937, Earhart aimed to set the record for flying around the world. The trip would consist of short flights covering long distances, with stopovers to refuel and rest. Her plan was to pilot her Lockheed aircraft while her navigator, an experienced pilot named Noonan, sat in the rear. For a while the trip went as planned.

70   Since Earhart and Noonan were unable to talk over the noise of the plane, they adopted a makeshift way to communicate. When Noonan consulted a map and wanted Earhart to make a turn, he'd write his directions on a piece of paper, stick it on the end of a long fishing pole, and push it to Earhart's side. She'd remove the slip of paper, nod, and turn left or right. Oddly enough, Earhart was
75 better able to communicate with the ground by using a two-way radio.

    In any case, Earhart was now en route. She had already made the 24th leg of the trip and had traveled 19,000 miles. Did the rest of the trip go smoothly? No. On July 2, 1937, on the 25th leg, disaster struck. The plane suddenly disappeared over the Pacific Ocean. Earhart and Noonan never landed in the South Pacific as planned.

80   President Roosevelt sent out a search party, but called it off after a week. Neither the bodies nor the plane were ever found. To this day, no one knows for sure what happened.

Where Did They Go?

    What went wrong? Some believe Earhart's aircraft ran out of fuel, crashed,
85 and fell into the ocean. Others have different theories, though without physical **evidence** no one can be certain. People are left to wonder what happened.

    One thing is known, however. Amelia Earhart was a brave woman with a fearless spirit. True, she was the first woman to cross the Atlantic by plane. But she was more than that. She was a **trailblazer** in aviation and holds a prominent place
90 in the history of courageous women.

5. Besides her flying abilities, for what other things was Earhart famous?

_____

6. What is one theory about what happened to their plane?

_____

stopovers *(noun)*
  stops made during a journey

navigator *(noun)*
  someone who gives information to guide the pilot of an airplane or ship

leg *(noun)*
  one of several parts of a journey

After You Read

Build a robust vocabulary.

Writing Sentences   Write a complete sentence to respond to each of the following questions or statements. Use the underlined word in your answer. Use the definitions on page 75 to help you.

1. Tell about a time when you showed independence.

_____

2. Do you think that aviation has changed in the last 100 years?

_____

3. What kind of innovator do you admire?

_____

4. Name someone who was a trailblazer in his or her field.

_____

5. If a fire is raging, what is like?

_____

Sentence Completions   Complete each sentence using a word from the box.

advocate	**aviation**	**determination**	**distinguished**	**evidence**
foretell	**independence**	**innovator**	**raging**	**trailblazer**

1. Can you _____ a person's career from her early interests?

2. Mr. Smith is an _____ for passenger safety.

3. His _____ to succeed put him at the top of his field.

4. The police found physical _____ in the woods.

5. Dr. Wilson is a _____ professor of science at his university.

Word Building: Root Words   A **root word** is the main part of a word that contains its basic meaning. Prefixes and suffixes can be added to a root word to form a new word. For example, the word *visit* is the root word in *revisiting*.

Circle the root word in each word below. Then write another word that uses the same root word, but has a different prefix or suffix. Then write a sentence using the new word.

1. unkind: _____

_____

2. inspection: _____

_____

3. uncertain: _____

_____

4. painter: _____

_____

5. rewind: _____

_____

TIP: When you read, you may find some long words that you do not recognize. Look closely to see the root word, prefixes, or suffixes. Understanding these word parts may help you figure out the word.

Writing Activity   Write a short paragraph that correctly uses key vocabulary words to describe a means of transportation a person might use. Tell why that form of transportation is important to that person. Use at least four of the words from the list on page 75. Reread the definitions, if necessary.

_____

_____

_____

Think about your reading.

Check your comprehension.   Answer each question. If you don't know the answer, reread the lines in parentheses.

1. Why were articles written about Amelia Earhart in the 1920s and 1930s? (lines 4–8)

_____

2. What was Earhart's job on her first trip across the Atlantic? (lines 34–38)

_____

3. How did Earhart keep awake when she piloted the plane solo across the Atlantic? (lines 50–51)

_____

4. What did President Roosevelt do to find Earhart's missing plane? (line 80)

_____

Use reading skills: Draw conclusions.

As you read, you can often **draw conclusions** based on the facts stated in an article. To do that, you take note of the facts or details, add your personal knowledge, then form a conclusion.

Draw conclusions.   As you read "The Disappearance of Amelia Earhart" you learned facts about Earhart. You can add your personal knowledge to this information and draw conclusions about Earhart's personality or character.

Reread the following lines from the article.

> Earhart had to earn money for flying lessons. She got a job as a nurse's aide and later as a social worker. She saved her earnings and was able to afford flying lessons the following year, receiving instruction from a female pilot.

1. Why do you think Earhart had to earn money for her flying lessons?

   _____

2. What personality or character traits does a person have who works and saves money for something she wants badly?

   _____

3. What conclusion do you draw about Earhart's personality or character?

   _____

Use a graphic organizer.

In the chart below fill in the missing information to draw conclusions about Earhart's character. The conclusion is completed for you.

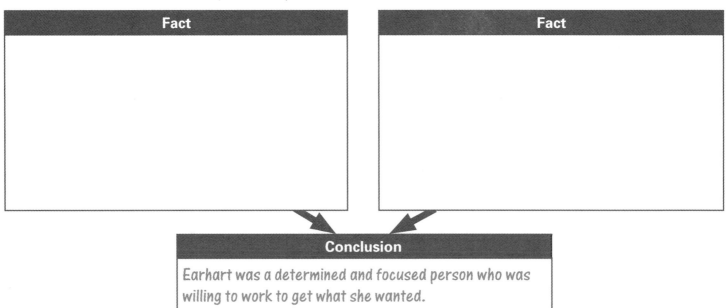

Fact	Fact

Conclusion

Earhart was a determined and focused person who was willing to work to get what she wanted.

Write about it.

Write a letter to the editor.

An editorial in a newspaper expresses an opinion. Imagine you are reading the newspaper in 1937. The following editorial expresses the writer's conclusion that Amelia Earhart was not a hero and that her final trip was a mistake:

> Those who think Amelia Earhart was a hero in 1937 are mistaken. Actually, she was foolish to attempt a trip around the world. She was an inexperienced pilot. Her plane was unsophisticated. She put her navigator Noonan at risk unnecessarily. She set back the field of aviation by decades when she disappeared into the ocean.

Respond to the editorial expressing your own conclusions about Earhart. Keep your letter short. Address your letter: "To the Editor." State the facts about Earhart as you know them and add your personal knowledge. Then state the conclusion you have drawn about Earhart and her trip.

Prewriting   On your own or with a partner, write the ideas that you will include. Fill in the graphic organizer to organize your thoughts.

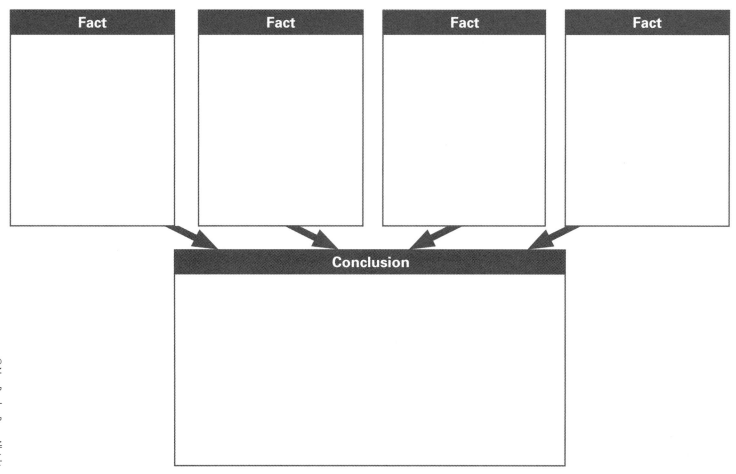

Thinking Beyond Reading   Think about these questions and discuss them with a partner. Add ideas to the graphic organizer as you talk.

- How would you describe Earhart's experience as a pilot?

- Do you think she was prepared for the trip around the world?

- Was Earhart responsible for the life of Noonan, her navigator?

- What conclusions have you reached about Earhart's trip?

- What conclusions have you reached about the editorial?

- Do you agree or not agree with the editorial?

Write a draft.   Write a first draft of your letter to the editor. Your letter might begin "To the Editor: I agree/disagree that Earhart's trip around the world was a foolish mistake." State the facts as you know them, then add your own personal knowledge. End your letter with a final statement that states your conclusion about Earhart. Use the ideas in your chart to help you write.

_____

_____

_____

_____

_____

_____

_____

_____

_____

_____

_____

_____

_____

Revise and create a final draft.   Write your final draft on a separate piece of paper. As you revise, check your draft for these specific points.

- Did you include facts in your letter?

- Did you clearly state your conclusion?

- Did you check spelling and grammar to make sure your writing is clear and correct?

Where Did That Fish Come From?

Learning Objectives

In this lesson you will:

■ Learn about a famous fish market.

■ Compare and contrast.

■ Master the key vocabulary used in the article.

■ Write a comparison.

Key Vocabulary

consumption *(noun)* the act of eating or drinking

distribution *(adjective)* supplying goods to customers in a particular area

established *(adjective)* well-known and proven

homespun *(adjective)* made at home

labor *(verb)* to work using a lot of physical effort

locale *(noun)* a place or location

maintenance *(adjective)* keeping a property in good condition

patrons *(noun)* people who use a particular store, restaurant, or company

refrigerated *(adjective)* cold in order to stay fresh

sanitary *(adjective)* clean and not involving any danger to your health

Before You Read

Active readers think about what they already know before they start to read. You can ask yourself active reading questions such as: What is the topic, and what do I already know about it? If you connect what you read to what you already know, you are more likely to understand what you are reading. Another effective active reading strategy is to try to visualize, or make pictures in your mind of what is happening, as you read. This helps you relate to and remember what you are reading.

Use what you know.

1. What is your favorite seafood or fish dish?

   _____

   _____

   _____

2. Do you know people who don't like fish? Do you know why?

   _____

   _____

   _____

3. How do you think fish and seafood get to the stores or restaurants in your neighborhood?

   _____

   _____

   _____

THINK ABOUT IT

One of my favorite restaurants serves fresh fish every day. Does that mean that the fish I ate was swimming in the ocean just yesterday?

Visualize while you are reading.

1. Picture in your mind what the original Fulton Fish Market looked like. How do you think the new market is different? Describe the differences you picture.

   _____

   _____

   _____

THINK ABOUT IT

I know the original Fulton Fish Market was very old. I imagine that it was very old-fashioned looking.

Next Stop, Fulton Fish Market

Read the article to find out about a market that sells fish. Write down on notes new things you learn about fish markets.

What's your favorite thing to order when you eat out? A hamburger deluxe? A pizza with everything? How about fish?

Throughout the United States, millions of people order fresh fish every day, but few diners stop to think about how that fish got to the restaurant. For folks in New York, New Jersey, and Connecticut, the fish may very well have passed through one main **distribution** site—the new Fulton Fish Market.

The Fulton Fish Market is a large 400,000-square-foot building located in Hunts Point, a section of the South Bronx, in New York City. The Fulton Fish Market cost $86 million to build. Opened in 2005, the market operates Monday to Friday from 1 A.M. to 12 noon and sells all kinds of fish to restaurants, retailers , and wholesalers . So, for example, if a chef in New Jersey plans to offer baked halibut or grilled salmon on Friday night's menu, she probably visits the fish market early that morning to buy what she needs for Friday night's **patrons.**

State of the Art

The new Fulton Fish Market is in a modern indoor space that is kept at a cool 40-degree temperature. No longer do the fishermen bring in their morning catch. Trucks now rush freshly-caught fish to the market. Designed with a central passageway and two main aisles, the Market houses more than 35 seafood stands. Buyers walk the aisles, selecting fish from the vendors , picking up, say, ten pounds of tuna from one stand or 25 pounds of catfish from another.

Since it's cold at the market, workers dress in sweaters and coats year round. It's not unusual to see a vendor bundled up in a hooded sweatshirt and a wool hat even in the summer. Individuals who visit the site (it costs $5.00

retailers *(noun)*
those who sell goods to the public

wholesalers *(noun)*
those who sell goods to retailers or other merchants

vendors *(noun)*
sellers

25 to get in) are not surprised to spot any number of the 600 employees with
fishhooks peaking out from their back pockets. Ten **maintenance** workers **labor**
to keep the place clean and **sanitary.** They do their jobs so well that one buyer
told a reporter, "You can lick off the floor almost."

Thursdays and Fridays are the busiest days at the market, as buyers purchase
larger amounts of fish for the weekend. Tuesdays and Wednesdays are quieter.

1. At what temperature is the new Fulton Fish Market kept?

_____

2. Who keeps the market clean and sanitary?

_____

Continue reading the article to find out where the old Fulton Fish Market was
located. Underline the sentences that tell you.

From Sea to Store

30 How does the fish, which swim in oceans and fish farms from Florida
to Maine, actually get to the market? It arrives there by truck. As many as
30 semi-trailers can be seen at any given time unloading their fish.

In a region as large as the northeast, and with a city as large as New York,
35 there are thousands of stores and restaurants into which the fish is sold. As
a result, the market deals with over 200 million pounds of seafood a year, an
amount worth half a billion dollars. Clearly, the Fulton Fish Market is big
business. And it's growing. Said one vendor, "People found out that fish is
healthy food, so more customers are ordering it in restaurants."

40 "It's true," said a restaurant owner. "I put a fish dish on the menu that
gets sold out every weekend." The dish, called Grilled Salmon, is made with
salmon, white wine, and herbs. It's so good that his regular customers ask for it
even when it's not on the menu.

While most fish sold at the market is from the United States, some vendors
45 have recently started flying in fish from the Caribbean, with success. Most
popular among these are parrotfish, from Antigua, and a fish from the Amazon
which tastes like pork.

Memories

For over 160 years, the original Fulton Fish Market was housed in lower
50 Manhattan, on, no surprise, Fulton Street, at the South Street Seaport.
The site was different from the space it's in now, and many employees and
customers look back fondly at its former **locale.**

The original market was outdoors. Workers labored in the snow, the hail,
and under the heat of the morning summer sun. Comparing the present indoor
55 space with its former outdoor home, one seller said, "I don't see the sunrise
anymore, but when it's raining, it's still bright inside."

3. Why is the number of people eating fish growing?

_____

4. Do workers prefer the new or the old market? Why?

_____

Finish reading the article to find out other ways the new market differs from the old one. Underline or highlight the sentences that tell you.

While conditions at the former location may sound more challenging than those at the present market, many workers look back at the former place with fondness. They say that the old market had character, while the present
60 place does not. True, it was still a business back then, but the everyday-people who shopped there gave it a **homespun** feel. For years, many housewives bought fish for their families there. In fact, a radio show aired from the South Street Seaport location in the 1940s. The show opened with *Good morning, housewives*, and signed off with a fish recipe.
65   If so many people loved the old site, why did the market move? There are many reasons. One has to do with food safety. In the old market, the fish sat outdoors on ice, putting it at risk of spoiling, while at the new site, the fish is kept **refrigerated.**

Other reasons concern practicality. The old spot was hard to reach by truck
70 while the new place is convenient to **established** truck routes. There is also the speed of unloading the fish. With more room in the new spot, trucks filled with fish get unloaded more quickly than before. And the new location has more storage space.

Perhaps the foremost reason concerns the new neighborhood. The South
75 Bronx, 13 miles from the old site, is a neighborhood with low-income families. People there need jobs. The point of opening the market in the South Bronx was to revitalize the area.

Whatever the future brings, one thing is for sure. Over the past few years, there has been a steady increase in seafood **consumption** in the United States.
80 That means that more diners will be lifting their forks to fish dishes when they sit down in restaurants or at their dinner tables. And that can only mean strong sales at the new Fulton Fish Market in the Bronx.

> **revitalize** *(verb)*
> to make something
> strong again

5. Why is fish safer at the new market?

_____

6. What are the five reasons the market moved to a new space?

_____

After You Read

Build a robust vocabulary.

Writing Sentences   Write a complete sentence to respond to each of the following questions or statements. Use the underlined word in your answer. Use the definitions on page 85 to help you.

1. Name a <u>sanitary</u> place or thing.

    _____

2. Name some foods that need to be <u>refrigerated</u>.

    _____

3. What job requires people to <u>labor</u> hard?

    _____

4. Who does the <u>maintenance</u> work in your apartment or house?

    _____

5. Describe a time you spoke with other <u>patrons</u> at a restaurant.

    _____

Sentence Completions   Complete each sentence using a word from the box.

consumption	distribution	established	homespun	labor
locale	maintenance	patrons	refrigerated	sanitary

1. The old _____ center was located in the South Street Seaport.

2. The colonial dress on display was probably _____.

3. The _____ of the new market made it easier for trucks to get there.

4. Our _____ of fish has increased since our doctor told us to eat it more often.

5. John drives an _____ route to work.

Word Building   A **prefix** is the group of letters before a word that changes the word's meaning. For example, the prefix *semi-* means *half*. The word *semicircle* means *a half-circle*. Here are some other prefixes and their meanings.

Prefix	Meaning
multi-	many
bi-	twice, every two
inter-	between
pre-	before

Read the words in the box. Circle the prefixes. Check your answers with a partner.

| predetermined | biracial | intersection | multinational |

Add the prefix *multi-*, *bi-*, *inter-*, or *pre-* to the words in the sentences below. Use the context, or the words around the word, to tell which prefix to add.

1. We meet _____monthly, every other month.

2. Different clergy spoke at the _____faith meeting with people of all religious backgrounds.

3. The students were _____talented, top performers with years of experience in singing, dance, and theater.

4. The meal was _____cooked and ready before the dinner began.

TIP: Sometimes prefixes are added to a root that is not a whole word. The prefix *bi-* means "two." The word *biped* means "an animal that has two feet."

Writing Activity   Write a short paragraph that correctly uses key vocabulary words to tell about a place where you like to eat. Use at least four of the words from the list on page 85. Reread the definitions, if necessary.

_____

_____

_____

_____

Think about your reading.

Check your comprehension.   Answer each question. If you don't know the answer, reread the lines in parentheses.

1. Who goes to the new Fulton Fish Market? (lines 10–11)

_____

2. Why do many workers at the market dress in sweaters and hats? (lines 15–16)

_____

3. Why are some customers ordering more fish in restaurants? (lines 38–39)

_____

4. Who has benefited from the new Fulton Fish Market's move to the Bronx? (lines 74–77)

_____

Use reading skills: Compare and contrast.

When you read, sometimes you notice comparisons and contrasts. When you **compare** things, you tell how they are alike. When you **contrast** things, you tell how they are different.

Compare and contrast.   As you read "Next Stop, Fulton Fish Market," you learned about the new and the old Fulton Fish Markets. Read the following paragraphs.

> If so many people loved the old site, why did the market move? There are many reasons. One has to do with food safety. In the old market, the fish sat outdoors on ice, putting it at risk of spoiling, while at the new site, the fish is kept refrigerated.
>
> Other reasons concern practicality. The old spot was hard to reach by truck while the new place is convenient to established truck routes. There is also the speed of unloading the fish. With more room in the new spot, trucks filled with fish get unloaded more quickly than before. And the new location has more storage space.

Contrast the conditions at the old and new Fulton Fish Markets.

1. What were conditions like at the old market?

   _____

   _____

2. What are conditions like at the new market?

   _____

   _____

Use a graphic organizer.

You can use a Venn diagram like the one below to compare and contrast. Fill in information about the conditions at the original Fulton Fish Market and the new indoor market.

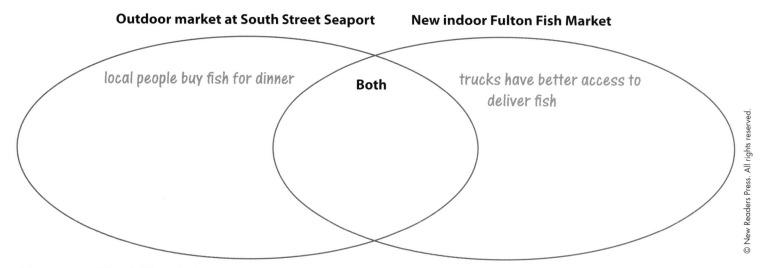

Outdoor market at South Street Seaport   **New indoor Fulton Fish Market**

local people buy fish for dinner   **Both**   trucks have better access to deliver fish

Write about it.

Write a comparison.

On your own or with a partner, brainstorm a list of old buildings or spaces that were replaced by something newer and perhaps better. Think about places in your community, schools that you attended, or businesses that have opened or closed. Write a comparison of the old place and the new one.

Prewriting   On your own or with a partner, choose one of the places from your list. Think about the ways in which the old and new places are different from each other. Consider the physical appearance, use of technology, accessibility, conveniences, and anything else you consider important or interesting. Think also about how they have remained the same. Use the graphic organizer to help you organize your ideas.

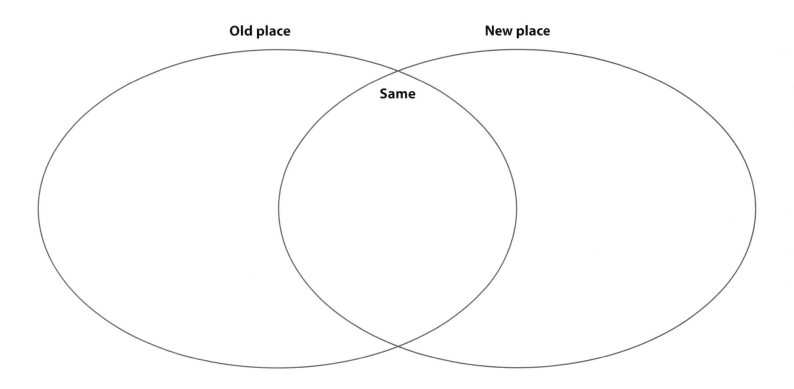

Old place   **New place**

Same

Thinking Beyond Reading   Think about these questions and discuss them with a partner. Add ideas to the graphic organizer as you talk.

• How important is it to remain comfortable with and fond of a place that you know well?

• How important is it to move forward with new places and improvements? Are there negative aspects to this type of thinking?

• How is a new place good for a community?

Write a draft.   Write a comparison of the new and old buildings or spaces you selected. Use the ideas in your diagram to help you write in a logical and organized way. Include as many details as you can think of. The reader would enjoy knowing which of the two you prefer.

_____

_____

_____

_____

_____

_____

_____

_____

_____

_____

_____

_____

_____

_____

Revise and create a final draft.   Write your final draft on a separate piece of paper. As you revise, check your draft for these specific points.

• Did you organize your ideas according to aspects of the buildings or places?

• Were you complete and balanced in comparing the institutions?

• Can the reader tell if you prefer the new or the old institution?

• Did you capitalize names of buildings and other places?

• Did you check spelling and grammar to make sure your writing is clear and correct?

Spending and Saving

Learning Objectives

In this lesson you will:

▨ Learn about how to become a good grocery shopper.

▨ Classify information you read.

▨ Master the key vocabulary used in the article.

▨ Write a description.

Key Vocabulary

analyze *(verb)* to study closely by separating into parts

contaminated *(adjective)* unfit to consume or ruined

expiration *(adjective)* the last time something can or should be used

imperfections *(noun)* defects

impulse *(adjective)* a sudden urge to do something

logic *(noun)* reasoned and careful thought

perimeter *(noun)* outside boundary or edge

spontaneous *(adjective)* arising from a momentary impulse

substantial *(adjective)* significant; great

venturing *(verb)* proceeding in the face of danger

Before You Read

The article you are about to read is about grocery shopping. This is a topic everyone knows something about. Think about what you know and how you feel about grocery shopping. Then scan the article, looking at the title and subheadings to see what you can expect and how the article is organized. These active reading strategies will help you to prepare to read the article and to get the most out of it.

Use what you know.

1. Have you ever gone grocery shopping?

   _____

   _____

   _____

My sister and I go grocery shopping together. We try to get out of there as fast as possible. I wonder what it would take to enjoy grocery shopping.

2. What do you like about grocery shopping?

   _____

   _____

   _____

3. What do you dislike about grocery shopping?

   _____

   _____

   _____

Preview before you read.

1. Read the title of the article. What can you expect to learn from reading the article?

   _____

   _____

   _____

Maybe the article will give me some ideas to save money and time. I might learn to shop more wisely.

2. Read the subheadings. What three topics about grocery shopping will the article cover?

   _____

   _____

   _____

Be a Better Grocery Shopper

Read the following article to find out what you should know to be a good shopper. Highlight or mark any tips that you think will help you shop.

"I put off grocery shopping to the last minute because I hate it," said Kathy Johnson. "I always end up on the longest checkout line. And I forget something each time I go."

Does Kathy's experience sound familiar? Do you avoid grocery shopping, too? Many Americans can save time and money, and shop more wisely, if they follow a few simple tips.

Save Time

Saving time at the grocery store actually begins at home. Before you leave for the store, decide what meals you will prepare for the week. Then make a list of the items you need. It's best to group things the way they are sold in the store—by dairy, produce, meat, household items, and so on.

At the store, cross off each item as you put it in your cart. If you use discount coupons, keep them clipped to your shopping list so they'll be available at the checkout line. Better yet, write your list on the back of an envelope and insert the coupons inside. On your shopping list put a check mark to remind yourself that you have a discount coupon for the item.

Grocery shopping during off-peak hours will shorten the trip. You'll save time if you shop between 10 A.M. and 4 P.M. weekdays, late at night, or early on Sunday mornings when it's less crowded. Avoid the after-work rush hours from 5 P.M. until about 8 P.M. when grocery stores are busiest.

Did you know that most large grocery stores are organized with fresh foods—such as fruits, vegetables, raw meat, seafood, and dairy products—on the **perimeter** of the store, and prepared foods—canned fruits and vegetables, packaged foods—

discount *(adjective)*
less than full price

off-peak *(adjective)*
not during the busiest time

25 in the middle? The outer aisles are generally roomier and less crowded than the middle. So you can cut your shopping time if you start on the perimeter—picking up tomatoes and lettuce—then **venturing** into the middle aisles, where you'll find bread, canned food, and nuts.

1. Which days and times can be classified as off-peak at a grocery store?

_____

_____

2. How do most grocery stores organize the food they sell?

_____

_____

Continue reading the article to find four tips on how to save money at the grocery store. Underline the sentences that state the four tips.

Save Money

30 The best way to save money is to create a food budget. First, **analyze** your spending on groceries. Figure out how much money you're actually spending on food. You can do this by saving your grocery receipts for a month, then finding the total. Decide how much you want to trim from that amount and which items can go. For example, if you notice that you're spending $16 per month on prepared foods like seafood salad, you can decide to make the foods at home. Preparing foods
35 yourself rather than buying them already-made will result in **substantial** savings.

Many of us add to our grocery bills when we give in to **impulse** buying, that is, to making **spontaneous** purchases. Sometimes, we make impulse purchases if we go to the store hungry. We grab the first thing we see that looks good, like candy or a sandwich, resulting, some experts report, in an increase in spending of up to
40 15 percent. To avoid impulse buying, eat *before* you enter the store. You'll stand a better chance of filling your cart with foods that are cost effective.

Another way to save money is to take only the cash that you'll need to pay for the groceries you're buying. While at home, scan your list and estimate the total. Then put only that amount in your wallet. Without extra spending money, you
45 won't be tempted to make unnecessary and often expensive purchases.

Comparison-shopping is an excellent way to reduce your food bill. When you comparison-shop, you compare two or more items to see which costs less, especially if two similar items come in different sizes or different brands . Use the unit price , often posted on a sticker under the item on the shelf, to figure out the
50 better buy. The unit price may be stated per ounce, pound, quart, or gallon.

3. How might you save money if you eat before you go to the grocery store?

_____

_____

brands (noun)
   products identified by the names of particular companies

unit price (noun)
   the cost for a single thing or part of the whole

4. Why is the tip on taking only the cash you need placed in the "Save Money" section of the article?

_____

_____

Finish reading the article to find tips on buying groceries wisely.

Let's look at an example. Pedro was in the market to buy a cake. "Which is the cheaper one?" he wondered as he looked at two different cakes. Pedro noticed that both cakes cost the same amount, but they were different sizes. **Logic** would tell Pedro that if he gets more for the same price, the larger item is the better buy. In
55 addition, Pedro looked at the unit prices on the shelf. The unit price for Brand 1 is lower, so the better buy is Brand 1. The unit price helped Pedro make his decision.

When you compare prices, be aware that stores often place the more expensive items at eye level and the lower priced items on a higher or lower shelf. So it's important to look up and down when shopping for the best deal. Also, the store
60 brand is often a few pennies cheaper than the national brands.

Other Ways to Buy Wisely

As intelligent shoppers, we want to keep our families and ourselves healthy and safe. This is especially important with perishable foods, such as fish, milk or meat, which can spoil and cause food poisoning. Try to keep perishable items cold.
65 When you get home, refrigerate or freeze them immediately.

perishable (adjective)
likely to spoil or decay

Did you know that most perishable items are stamped with an **expiration** date? That is the last date by which a food should be eaten. Check the date before buying, and throw out any item from your refrigerator if that date has passed.

When shopping for eggs, open the carton in the store and check that none are
70 broken or cracked. Move each egg slightly to be sure it's not stuck. You don't want to break an egg as you remove it from the carton. That would be wasteful.

As you shop for canned goods, look for dents or leaks. Avoid any item with damage or **imperfections,** since the food inside may be **contaminated.**

By following these tips, you can spend less time and money at the grocery
75 store and make wiser purchases for your family. Said one man from Los Angeles, "I started shopping early on weekend mornings. And I bring only the cash I need to buy what's on my list. Grocery shopping is a lot less painful to me now."

5. Why should you put perishable items in your shopping cart last?

_____

_____

6. Do you think the paragraph on looking for dents in cans belongs in the "Other Ways to Buy Wisely" section of the article? Explain.

_____

_____

After You Read

Build a robust vocabulary.

Writing Sentences Write a complete sentence to respond to each of the following questions or statements. Use the underlined word in your answer. Use the definitions on page 95 to help you.

1. Tell about a <u>spontaneous</u> decision you made to do something.

   _____

2. What <u>imperfections</u> have you noticed in your home?

   _____

3. What is the <u>logic</u> of comparison shopping?

   _____

4. What kind of <u>impulse</u> buying do you do?

   _____

5. Tell what you find in the <u>perimeter</u> of your grocery store.

   _____

Sentence Completions Complete each sentence using a word from the box.

analyze	contaminated	expiration	imperfections	impulse
logic	perimeter	spontaneous	substantial	venturing

1. When he went hiking, Jeff was _____ into new territory.

2. The robbers stole a _____ amount of money from the bank.

3. To see if you're overspending, _____ your last four grocery receipts.

4. Everyone needs to avoid _____ food.

5. What is the _____ date on the cottage cheese?

Word Building Suffixes A **suffix** is a group of letters added to the end of a word. When a suffix is added, a new word with a new meaning is formed. The suffix *-scope* means view. A *telescope* is an instrument for viewing things far away. Here are two other suffixes and their meanings.

Suffix	Meaning
-ship	a state of being
-less	without

Circle the suffix in each word. Write the meaning. Then write a sentence using the word.

1. microscope: _____

_____

2. fearless: _____

_____

3. relationship: _____

_____

4. clueless: _____

_____

5. friendship: _____

_____

TIP: When you read, you may notice words with suffixes. If you remember what the suffix means, you can probably figure out the meaning of the word.

Writing Activity   Write a short paragraph that correctly uses key vocabulary words to tell about how to save time or money on a household chore. Use at least four of the words from the list on page 95. Reread the definitions, if necessary.

_____

_____

_____

Think about your reading.

Check your comprehension.   Answer each question. If you don't know the answer, reread the lines in parentheses.

1. What can you do at home to save time when you get to a grocery store? (lines 8–11)

_____

2. How are most grocery stores organized? (lines 21–24)

_____

3. Why should you bring only the cash you need to make grocery purchases? (lines 44–45)

_____

4. What is the first thing to do at home with perishable items? (lines 64–65)

_____

Using Reading Skills: Classify

When you **classify,** you think how ideas are related and why they belong together. Often an author classifies for you, organizing an article in sections of related ideas. If you understand how the article's ideas are classified, it will help you remember and understand what you read.

Classify information.   As you read "Be a Better Grocery Shopper," you probably noticed that the author organized her information into three main sections: "Save Time," "Save Money," and "Other Ways to Buy Wisely." The ideas in each section are related.

Reread the following two paragraphs from the section called "Other Ways to Buy Wisely."

> When shopping for eggs, open the carton in the store and check that none are broken or cracked. Move each egg slightly to be sure it's not stuck. You don't want to break an egg as you remove it from the carton. That would be wasteful.
>
> As you shop for canned goods, look for dents or leaks. Avoid any item with damage or imperfections, since the food inside may be contaminated.

1. When shopping, why should you open a carton of eggs before buying it?

   _____

2. Why should you look at the outside of a can before buying it?

   _____

3. What is the same about checking an egg carton and checking a can? How are the ideas related?

   _____

4. Besides "Other Ways to Buy Wisely," what is another good category name for this section?

   _____

Use a graphic organizer.

You can use a graphic organizer like the one below to help you classify information. Fill in the tips the author gives in the article for each heading. You may want to review the article before you begin.

Shopping Tips

Save Time	Save Money	Other Ways to Buy Wisely

Write about it.

Write a description.

When you write a description, you include specific details that help the reader form a picture in his or her mind. You will write a description of a drugstore, hardware store, garden center, or some other kind of store. Tell what the main departments or sections are in the store and what kinds of things you find in each one.

Prewriting   On your own or with a partner, organize the ideas that you will include in your description by using the graphic organizer below. Label the columns with the name of the department or sections in the store. Then fill in each column with the kinds of things you find in that department or section. You may not need all of the columns, or you may need to add more.

Thinking Beyond Reading Think about these questions and discuss them with a partner. Add ideas to the graphic organizer as you talk.

- How is the store laid out?

- What do you see when you first enter the store?

- Are some departments or sections bigger than others?

- Are there signs for each department?

Write a draft. Write a first draft of your description. Be sure to begin by naming the kind of store you are describing. Include the names of each department or section and what it looks like, including the kinds of items that are found there.

_____

_____

_____

_____

_____

_____

_____

_____

_____

_____

_____

_____

_____

_____

Revise and create a final draft. Write your final draft on a separate piece of paper. As you revise, check your draft for these specific points.

- Did you name the kind of store?

- Did you describe the various departments and what they are like?

- Did you check spelling and grammar to make sure your writing is clear and correct?

Answer Key

Lesson 1 Staying Fit and Healthy
pp. 5–14

Writing Sentences

Sample answers:

1. Derek Jeter and LeBron James are two sports <u>icons</u> of today.

2. I had an <u>obsession</u> about keeping my car clean.

3. I was <u>ecstatic</u> when our team won the championship.

4. I go to the dentist <u>faithfully</u>.

5. If you are <u>contorting</u> your face, it looks wrinkled and scary.

Sentence Completions

1. smirk

2. specimens

3. unaccountable

4. surveyed

5. inwardly

Word Building

Sample answers:

1. surprised: Joe surprised his wife with a beautiful diamond pin.

2. waved: They waved goodbye from the train.

3. visited: We visited our cousins in Mexico.

4. clapped: Everyone clapped when the symphony ended.

5. missed: Ernie was late and missed the bus.

Writing Activity

Answers will vary. Review the vocabulary words and the definitions. Find the words in the article to make sure they are used correctly.

Check your comprehension.

Sample answers:

1. Tim wants to find out how to get the steroids Ox uses.

2. He feels his muscles grow.

3. Ox tells Tim about roid rage and acne.

4. Tim begins to think Ox is right because he has acne and has been very angry.

Make Inferences

Sample answers:

1. Inference: Steroids help build muscle.

2. Inference: Paul sells very effective steroids.

Use a graphic organizer.

Sample answers:

1. What you know: He's taking steroids.

2. Inference you make: The steroids are making him happy.

3. What you know: Steroids change people's behavior.

4. Inference you make: Tim is feeling the effects of steroids.

Prewriting

Sample answers:

Center circle: Steroids should be banned for recreational athletes. Surrounding circles: They are dangerous; They have side effects; It's not fair if some athletes use them and some don't.

Thinking Beyond Reading

The graphic organizer might now include more reasons why steroids should be banned.

Write a draft.

Your first draft might begin with a sentence that tells your own point of view. Use the details in your chart to support your letter.

Revise and create a final draft.

The final draft should include good arguments to support your own point of view. Sentences should be complete and use correct spelling and punctuation.

Lesson 2 On the Job
pp. 15–25

Writing Sentences

Sample answers:

1. I felt <u>lethargic</u> after eating a big holiday meal.

2. An old winter coat might be <u>threadbare</u>.

3. I once <u>confronted</u> my brother about his messy habits.

4. Deciding whether or not to leave my last job was a <u>dilemma</u>.

5. Yes, I can <u>recite</u> the Pledge of Allegiance.

Sentence Completions

1. engulfing

2. jeopardize

3. surreptitiously

4. sauntered

5. condone

Word Building

Sample answers:

1. knives: Please put the steak knives in the drawer.

2. loaves: Mom baked three loaves of bread.

3. halves: We'll cut the apples into halves.

4. calves: All the calves are growing well.

5. wharves: Seaports have many wharves where ships can dock.

Writing Activity

Answers will vary. Review the vocabulary words and the definitions. Find the words in the story to make sure they are used correctly.

Check your comprehension.

Sample answers:

1. They went to school together and lived in the same building.

2. Richard stood up for Marco with the boss. He worried about Marco, too.

3. Marco could have gotten another job and not stolen the tips.

4. No, Richard says he will never work with Marco again.

Make judgments.

Sample answers:

1. Richard saw Marco steal money from the tip box.

2. Marco is a dishonest person and can't be trusted.

Use a graphic organizer.

Sample answer:

My judgment: Marco is untrustworthy and doesn't deserve Richard's friendship.

Prewriting

Sample answers:

I know: The cook may have bad motives. The restaurant needs proof that Jack stole.

My judgment: Jack is innocent until proven guilty.

Thinking Beyond Reading

The graphic organizer might now include more explanation of the issue and more details that support your opinion.

Write a draft.

Use the ideas in your chart to write your paragraph. State your judgment at the end.

Revise and create a final draft.

The final draft should include a clear statement of your judgment of what the restaurant should do. Sentences should be complete and use correct spelling and punctuation.

Lesson 3 We Are Family
pp. 26–36

Writing Sentences

Sample answers:

1. I felt <u>anxiety</u> when I had to take my driving test.

2. You can become <u>financially</u> secure by saving your money in an IRA.

3. I am <u>unique</u> because I am the only person in my family with red hair.

4. I reacted <u>emotionally</u> at my son's wedding.

5. Noisy neighbors and the leak in my bathroom sink are <u>aggravations</u>.

Sentence Completions

1. status

2. extensive

3. resolve

4. socializing

5. stigma

Word Building

Circle: *adjust, frustrat, like, visit, present.*

Sample answers:

1. adjusted: We adjusted our seatbelts before the plane took off.

2. frustrated: Hank was frustrated when he couldn't hit the ball.

3. disliked: We disliked the food at the new restaurant downtown.

4. revisit: Can we revisit that topic at a later time?

5. presentable: Sarah looked very presentable at her interview.

Writing Activity

Answers will vary. Review the vocabulary words and their definitions. Find the words in the article to see how they are used.

Check your comprehension.

Sample answers:

1. Over 17% had an only child.

2. A major reason is the high divorce rate.

3. There is very little difference.

4. They worry that their kids are lonely.

Synthesize information.

Sample answers:

1. Some parents worry that their child is lonely.

2. They take their child to day care, involve their child in sports teams or play-dates, or sign their child up for classes.

3. Parents relieve their anxiety by setting up opportunities for their children to socialize.

Use a graphic organizer.

Sample answers:

2. They involve their childen in sports teams.

3. They sign up their children for classes.

Synthesize the information: There are many ways for onlies to meet other children and not be lonely.

Prewriting

Answers will vary but might look like this.

2. What I know: Children visit another child's home on a play date. Suggestions and benefits: Caroline will learn to feel comfortable away from home and possibly make a close friend.

3. What I know: Lots of kids love to run around after school. It's healthy for them to be active. Suggestions and benefits: Have Caroline join a soccer team. She'll make new friends and the exercise will be good for her.

Thinking Beyond Reading

Your graphic organizer might now include more ways for Caroline to socialize and make friends.

Write a draft.

Use the details in your chart to write your explanation.

Revise and create a final draft.

The final draft should include ideas to support your suggestions. Sentences should be complete and use correct spelling and punctuation.

Lesson 4 Making a Comeback
pp. 37–47

Writing Sentences

Sample answers:

1. My children are <u>dependent</u> on me.

2. A baby who is <u>thriving</u> would be growing well.

3. A person who salutes the flag shows she is <u>patriotic</u>.

4. When I was growing up, money was <u>scarce</u> in my family.

5. Bringing out a cake with candles can <u>energize</u> a birthday party.

Sentence Completions

1. abandoned

2. revenue

3. flourished

4. experimental

5. complex

Word Building

Circle *mis-, re-, un-, im-.*

Sample answers:

1. mis-

2. un-

3. re-

4. im-

5. un-

Writing Activity

Answers will vary. Review the vocabulary words and the definitions. Find the words in the article to make sure they are used correctly.

Check your comprehension.

Sample answers:

1. The closing left some people unemployed.

2. It gave people jobs and things to do.

3. The town went downhill. Banks closed. People couldn't afford homes.

4. The museum attracted people and money to North Adams.

Identify main idea and details.

Sample answers:

1. Residents of North Adams were worried.

2. Where would they find jobs? Would they have to move to find work?

Use a graphic organizer.

Sample answers:

Main Idea: Sprague added to the energy of the town in more ways than one.

Supporting Details: The electric company operated 24 hours a day. The company played patriotic songs.

Prewriting

Sample answers:

Main Idea: I was mugged in the park.

Supporting Detail: I was alone at night.

Supporting Detail: It happened when I was 21, two years ago.

Thinking Beyond Reading

The graphic organizer might now include more details about the event and its effect on you.

Write a draft.

Use the ideas in your chart to write your paragraph. State your main idea and give details to support it.

Revise and create a final draft.

The final draft should include a clear statement of your main idea as well as supporting details. Sentences should be complete and use correct spelling and punctuation.

Lesson 5 Summer Vacations
pp. 48–58

Writing Sentences

Sample answers:

1. My morning <u>routine</u> includes drinking coffee and reading the paper.

2. People often dance the hula at a <u>luau</u>.

3. I <u>relish</u> sleeping late on the weekend.

4. Global warming is an <u>environmental</u> problem we have.

5. My girlfriend was <u>supportive</u> of me when I decided to go back to school.

Sentence Completions

1. exclusively

2. conventional

3. acquire

4. cater

5. bond

Word Building

Circle *ly, ly, ful, ness, al.*

Sample answers:

1. I'm not sure I fully understand your question.

2. Ben happily handed in his final homework assignment.

3. Jackie showed she is thoughtful by helping the old man across the street.

4. She showed her kindness by babysitting for the infant.

5. That is an original painting by a great artist.

Writing Activity

Answers will vary. Review the vocabulary words and the definitions. Find the words in the article to see how they are used.

Check your comprehension.

Sample answers:

1. They give children a chance to bond with others while learning sports, art, music, or school subjects in a natural environment.

2. It's only for children with parents in the military.

3. They might bring Camp-in-a-Suitcase to them.

4. Camp promotes physical, social, emotional, and academic growth.

Identify fact and opinion.

Underline *Andrea sent 13 postcards.*

Circle *Every child should have a chance to go to camp.*

Use a graphic organizer.

Sample answers:

2. Fact: Before Donna got on the camp bus, she didn't talk.
   Opinion: Donna's counselors were great.

3. Fact: After two weeks at camp, Mike was calmer.
   Opinion: Camp was a positive experience.

4. Fact: Teisha used to slouch a lot.
   Opinion: Camp was wonderful.

Prewriting

Answers will vary but might include:

Facts: There are camps for kids like Max. The counselors will be there to make sure he is safe.

Opinions: Every child should have a chance to go to camp. Camp is wonderful.

Thinking Beyond Reading

The graphic might now include more facts and opinions about sending Max to camp.

Write a draft.

Your paragraph might begin with a topic sentence like this: "I know that you are thinking of sending Max to summer camp." Use the ideas in your chart to write your description. State your opinion at the end.

Revise and create a final draft.

The final draft should include facts and opinions that support your position on whether or not Max should go to camp. Sentences should be complete and use correct spelling and punctuation.

Lesson 6 Help in an Emergency
pp. 59–68

Writing Sentences

Sample answers:

1. A <u>dilemma</u> I faced was whether to spend time with my friends or my boyfriend.

2. You might see smoke <u>spewing</u> from a factory smokestack.

3. I <u>grimaced</u> when I tasted a lemon.

4. I might speak to someone <u>tersely</u> if I was in a hurry.

5. People rushing in late can cause a <u>commotion</u>.

Sentence Completions

1. disoriented
2. engulfed
3. potentially
4. maneuvering
5. maelstrom

Word Building

kick/board, law/breaker, sand/blast, in/land

Sample answers:

1. someone who fights fires; The firefighter was very brave.
2. a bomb that causes fire; The protester threw a firebomb.
3. wood that can be burned to make a fire; We need more firewood.
4. a wall that stops fire; There were no firewalls in place.
5. an intense fire that creates wind; The firestorm overwhelmed the firefighters.

Writing Activity

Answers will vary. Review the vocabulary words and the definitions. Find the words in the story to make sure they are used correctly.

Check your comprehension.

Sample answers:

1. It took the truck a long time to reach the fire because it came from a long way away.
2. The captain tells the firefighters not to put water on the fires because he doesn't know if the water will put out the fire or fuel it.
3. Pasquini faces the dilemma of putting himself in danger to get the people or staying safe until the hazmat team arrives.
4. Pasquini says he rescued the workers because it's "what we do."

Identify cause and effect.

Sample answers:

1. They moaned.
2. The men wearing them ran when they heard the explosion.

Use a graphic organizer.

Sample answers:

1. The explosion
2. The fire is at a chemical plant.
3. Pasquini goes in to rescue the workers.

Prewriting

Answers will vary but may include: Middle—Pasquini and the other firefighters get to the fire and begin to fight it. End—Pasquini hears moans and goes into the fire to rescue two workers.

Thinking Beyond Reading

Answers to the questions might include: Good firefighters need to be strong and brave; the firefighters used the right amount of caution before the hazmat truck got there; Pasquini made a good choice because he stayed safe and saved a worker.

Write a draft.

Use the ideas in your chart to write your paragraph. Include the main events in the story.

Revise and create a final draft.

The final draft should include the main events that happened in the story in the order that they happened. Sentences should be complete and use correct spelling and punctuation.

Lesson 7 A Sports Icon
pp. 69–78

Writing Sentences

Sample answers:

1. I lost my <u>composure</u> last week when I yelled at my dog for barking too long.
2. I'd choose Oprah Winfrey to <u>mentor</u> me.
3. Working out at the gym requires <u>discipline</u>.
4. Chris Evert <u>dominated</u> women's tennis.
5. <u>Integrity</u> requires honesty.

Sentence Completions

1. promising
2. stamina
3. witnessed
4. prestigious
5. surpassing

Word Building

Sample answers:

Circle -er in all the words.

1. colder: In the mountains it's much colder at night than it is during the day.
2. funnier: I think that Jay Leno is funnier than David Letterman.
3. lighter: The 10-pound bag is lighter than the 20-pound bag.

4. heavier: In general, trucks are heavier than cars.

5. hotter: It's hotter today than it was yesterday.

Writing Activity

Answers will vary. Review the vocabulary words and the definitions. Find the words in the article to see how they are used.

Check your comprehension.

Sample answers:

1. While playing in his crib, he pretended to swing a golf club, and when he was 2 he showed off his golf swing on TV.

2. He improved his chances of becoming a world-class player by practicing a lot.

3. It taught Tiger concentration and composure.

4. He was the youngest player and the first player of African-American or Asian background to win it.

Recognize time order.

1. He won his first international junior golf competition.

2. He won again.

3. When he was 12, 13, 14, and 15 years old.

Use a graphic organizer.

Birth: b; School: a; College: e; Masters Championship: c; Adult: d

Prewriting

Decide which major developmental events should be in your time line. Write the dates and list them in time order. You can add more lines if you have more events.

Thinking Beyond Reading

Answers will vary, but might now include additional events or people that influenced this person's life.

Write a draft.

Your first draft might include the idea that this person is respected because of how different people and events influenced his or her life. Include the events from your time line to support your ideas.

Revise and create a final draft.

The paragraph should include a topic sentence and details to support the main idea. Sentences should be complete and use correct spelling and punctuation.

Lesson 8 Flying High
pp. 79–89

Writing Sentences

Sample answers:

1. I showed independence once when I went to a movie by myself.

2. Aviation has changed in many ways, including the size of planes, speed, and flight control information.

3. The kind of innovator I admire is an inventor like Thomas Edison or an artist like Picasso.

4. Martin Luther King, Jr., was a trailblazer in civil rights.

5. A fire that is raging is burning furiously and out of control.

Sentence Completions

1. foretell

2. advocate

3. determination

4. evidence

5. distinguished

Word Building

Sample answers:

1. Circle *kind,* kindness: I really appreciate your kindness.

2. Circle *inspect,* inspector: My cousin is a building inspector.

3. Circle *certain,* certainly: We will certainly go to the party.

4. Circle *paint,* repaint: We're going to have to repaint that wall.

5. Circle *wind,* winding: The politician is winding up his speech.

Writing Activity

Answers will vary. Review the vocabulary words and the definitions. Find the words in the article to make sure they are used correctly.

Check your comprehension.

Sample answers:

1. She was making history in aviation.

2. She kept the plane's log.

3. She used smelling salts.

4. He sent out a search party.

Draw conclusions.

Sample answers:

1. Probably her parents were not willing to pay for her lessons.

2. determination, ability to wait for a result, ability to plan for the future, willingness to work

3. Earhart was determined and independent.

Use a graphic organizer.

Sample answers:

Facts: Earhart worked hard. Earhart saved money.

Prewriting

Sample answers:

Facts: Earhart had gone on many flights before the trip around the world. She was an experienced and honored pilot. She had broken flying records and earned a variety of awards. The books she'd authored were well known.

Conclusion: Earhart's trip was not a mistake and she was a hero. She may have hit a storm or her map may have been incorrect. But the trip was well thought out.

Thinking Beyond Reading

Answers will vary but might include: She broke many records and did a lot of flying. Her experience was extensive. She seemed prepared for the trip around the world because she had made many shorter trips. Earhart and Noonan were equally responsible for the success of the trip. Earhart's trip brought more attention to the field of aviation. The editorial is wrong because the facts prove otherwise. It may be that the maps Noonan used were outdated or incorrect and they couldn't find where they were supposed to land.

Write a draft.

Use the ideas in your chart to write your paragraph. State your facts and your conclusion.

Revise and create a final draft.

The final draft should include a clear statement of your conclusion and the facts that lead you to it. Sentences should be complete and use correct spelling and punctuation.

Lesson 9 Where Did That Fish Come From? pp. 90–99

Writing Sentences

Sample answers:

1. An operating room in a hospital is a <u>sanitary</u> place.

2. Milk, butter, and eggs need to be <u>refrigerated</u>.

3. Road work requires people to <u>labor</u> hard.

4. My father does all the <u>maintenance</u> work at our house.

5. I once asked two restaurant <u>patrons</u> for the ketchup from their table.

Sentence Completions

1. distribution

2. homespun

3. locale

4. consumption

5. established

Word Building

Sample answers:

Circle *pre-, bi-, inter-, multi-*.

1. bi-

2. inter-

3. multi-

4. pre-

Writing Activity

Answers will vary. Review the vocabulary words and the definitions. Find the words in the article to see how they are used.

Check your comprehension.

Sample answers:

1. Chefs and fish wholesalers and retailers go to the market.

2. They wear sweaters because the temperature is 40 degrees.

3. Customers are ordering more fish because they learned that fish is healthy food.

4. People who live in the South Bronx have benefited from the move.

Compare and contrast.

Sample answers:

1. Fish was on ice and could spoil, hard to reach by truck, took longer to unload, not much storage space

2. Fish is refrigerated, convenient to truck routes, faster unloading, more storage space

Use a graphic organizer.:

Sample answers:

Outdoor market: outdoors, workers labored in all conditions, had character

New indoor market: indoors, modern, cool temperature all year, fish is safer, more storage space

Both: lots of really fresh fish, many vendors, retail and wholesale

Prewriting

The graphic organizer should include ideas that compare an old place to a new place. Places might be a new or renovated mall, city hall or library or police station, or a school that has been converted to another use.

Thinking Beyond Reading

Answers will vary, but might now include more ways in which the new and old places are the same or different.

Write a draft.

Your first draft might begin with a sentence, such as the following: "Our old comfortable library had served our community well for many years, but the new library is beautiful and offers many more services." Include the ideas from your graphic organizer.

Revise and create a final draft.

The paragraph should include a topic sentence and details to support the main idea. Sentences should be complete and use correct spelling and punctuation.

Lesson 10 Spending and Saving
pp. 100–110

Writing Sentences

Sample answers:

1. I recently made a <u>spontaneous</u> decision to go to a movie by myself.

2. Two <u>imperfections</u> I've noticed are chipped dishes and worn carpet.

3. The <u>logic</u> of comparison shopping is to identify the best buys.

4. I sometimes <u>impulse</u> buy junk food when I am very hungry.

5. Produce, meat, and dairy products are located around the <u>perimeter</u> of my grocery store.

Sentence Completions

1. venturing
2. substantial
3. analyze
4. contaminated
5. expiration

Word Building

Sample answers:

1. Circle -*scope,* an instrument for viewing things close up; A biologist often uses a microscope.

2. Circle -*less,* without fear; My brother is fearless.

3. Circle -*ship,* state of being related; I have a good relationship with my parents.

4. Circle -*less,* without a clue; Maria was clueless about how to act.

5. Circle -*ship,* state of being a friend; Your friendship is important to me.

Writing Activity

Answers will vary. Review the vocabulary words and the definitions. Find the words in the article to make sure they are used correctly.

Check your comprehension.

Sample answers:

1. You can make a shopping list at home.

2. Stores are organized with the fresh fruits and vegetables, fish, dairy products, and meat on the perimeter and other items in the middle.

3. You avoid impulse buying by bringing only the cash you need.

4. Refrigerate or freeze them right away.

Classify information.

Sample answers:

1. Open the eggs before buying them to be sure they aren't cracked.

2. Look at the outside of the can to be sure it's not dented.

3. They are both tips for buying wisely and keeping your family healthy.

4. Other names for the subhead might be: *Keep Them Healthy* or *Smart Shopping* or *Better Safe Than Sorry.*

Use a graphic organizer.

Sample answers:

Save time: write and use a shopping list, keep coupons handy, go at off-peak times.

Save money: create a budget, prepare food yourself, eat before you shop, take only as much cash as you need, comparison shop.

Other ways to buy wisely: Keep perishables cool and refrigerate them as soon as you get home, check expiration dates, check eggs for cracks, avoid damaged cans and packages.

Prewriting

Answers will vary but should include several departments or sections for the chosen store as well as items that can be found in them.

Thinking Beyond Reading

Answers will vary but should include where in the store each department is located, which ones you see first when you enter the store, what kind of sign or other label identifies each section.

Write a draft.

Use the ideas in your chart to write your description. State the kind of store and the way it is organized, including the kinds of items and where they're found.

Revise and create a final draft.

The final draft should describe the store so that the reader gets a good picture of the way it is organized. Sentences should be complete and use correct spelling and punctuation.